BASIC AVIATION MODELLING

Compendium Modelling Manuals
Volume 1

Series Editor: Jerry Scutts

D1227787

COMPENDIUM

Compendium Modelling Manuals

Basic Aviation Modelling

This edition published by Compendium Publishing Ltd,
5 Gerrard Street, London, W1V 7LJ

Printed in the UK
Designed by Compendium Design and Production

All rights reserved. No part of this publication may be
reproduced or transmitted in any form or by any means
electronic or mechanical including photocopy, recording, or in
any information storage and retrieval system, without the prior
written consent of the publishers.

A CIP catalogue record for this book is available from the
British Library

ISBN 1 902579 04 6

For further information about any other books in this series
please write to

The Sales Manager

Compendium Publishing, 5 Gerrard Street, London, W1V 7LJ
Tel   0171 287 4570
Fax 0171 494 0583

ttempt has been made to
fy the brands of paint used
ighout this book. The basic
s are, as indicated, much
he modeller's individual
ce based on local avail-
y of paints and inks as well
e reference material used.
es of oil-based enamel and
r-based acrylic paints and
suitable for use on poly-
ne plastic are available in
retail outlets in most
tries.

ASSEMBLY OF A PLASTIC KIT

One of the most popular aspects of modelling is that of constructing replicas of aeroplanes. In this first chapter we examine the secrets of good assembly of kit parts, attention to fine detail and the use of body putty. Painting with an airbrush will be touched upon and by following simple rules and with the appropriate use of materials and tools, we show how excellent results can be achieved by almost anyone, regardless of age.

In the succeeding chapters two skill levels in modelling will be covered and any difficult areas examined to overcome these. Initially we assume some experience of the hobby on the part of the reader and later on, some of the challenges faced by the beginner.

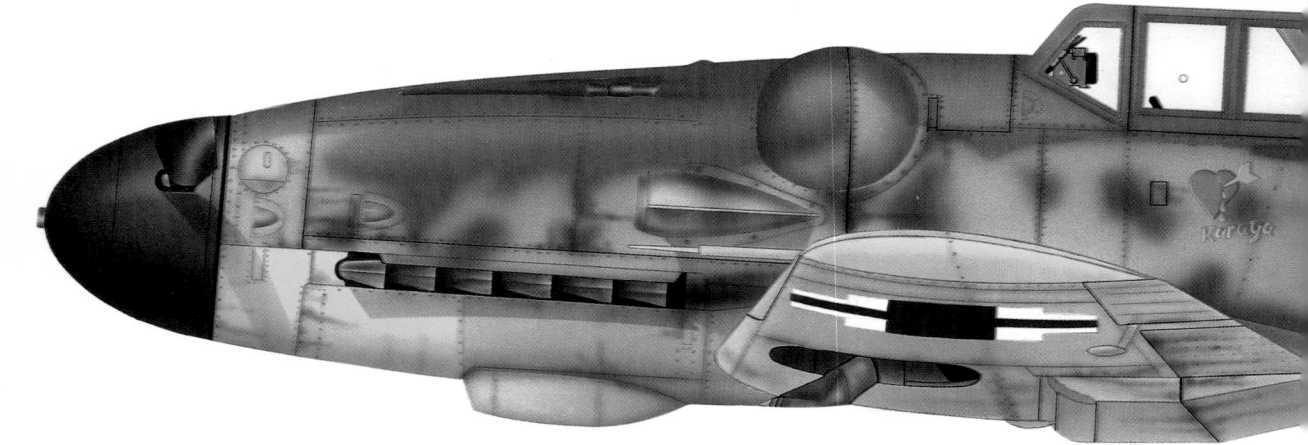

Once we have decided to assemble a kit of an aeroplane, different preferences in choosing one particular model come into play. While some people build models from all eras, others stay loyal to aircraft which have an intrinsic appeal as regards shape, those with history behind them or a special fondness stemming from having flown in that type, even as a mere passenger.

Having chosen the model to build, the second phase begins the search for the kit most suitable to the individual's skills. With a popular aircraft type, multiple kits will be available from a variety of manufacturers. The beginner would be wise to opt for the most economical kit, as a new modeller usually needs to work up to a good standard and should

A fine model of a Pitts biplane in 1/72 scale. It is shown at actual-size.

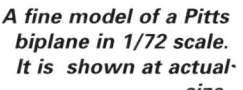

anticipate less than satisfying results from a few cheap kits before that goal is achieved.

That said, the most expensive kits are not necessarily the best. Therefore our task is to check to see that the component parts are 'flash' free with no 'sink' marks in the plastic surfaces, that there are no deformities in the moulded parts and that all sprues are complete. The choice of a kit is usually based on a quality/cost ratio so that in the event of the beginner spoiling a cheap model, it can easily be replaced.

CHOOSING THE SCALE

The first thing a modeller needs to know is what the term 'scale' means in other words that fraction that always appears on the kit box as the figure '1' followed by a colon or oblique mark. It means simply that the model has been scaled down from the original machine a specific number of times: a scale of 1/100 therefore indicates that the

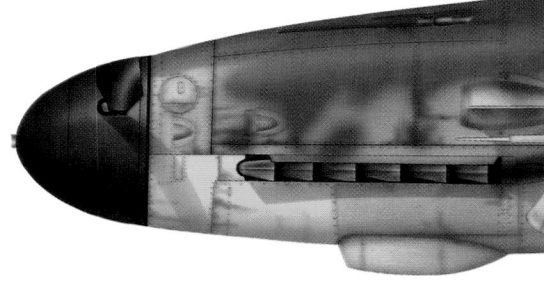

model has been reduced 100 the scale of 1/72, seventy-two and so forth. The smaller th able figure, the larger the size model. Knowing these scale is useful in two ways: f enables the modeller to different kits to a constant, rable size which is part important when const dioramas, and secondly to that the manufacturers have out the dimensions of the original accurately. With data to hand, only a simple sion sum will be necessary to mine the correct proportions model.

There are three most con used scales – 1/72, 1/48 and 1/ first of these is the most distributed with hundreds o able kits from a large num

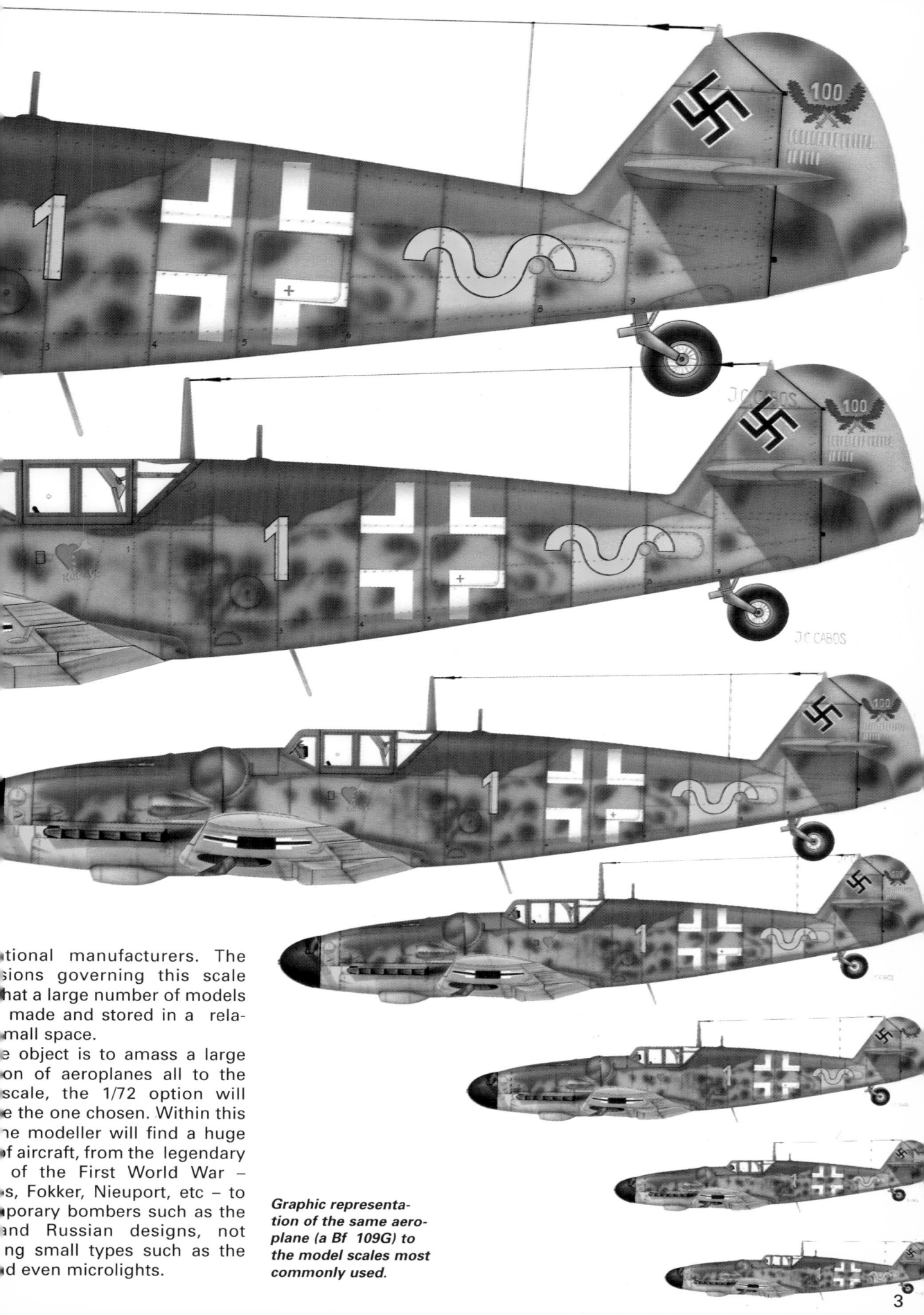

tional manufacturers. The
sions governing this scale
hat a large number of models
made and stored in a rela-
mall space.

e object is to amass a large
on of aeroplanes all to the
scale, the 1/72 option will
e the one chosen. Within this
he modeller will find a huge
f aircraft, from the legendary
of the First World War –
s, Fokker, Nieuport, etc – to
porary bombers such as the
nd Russian designs, not
ng small types such as the
d even microlights.

*Graphic representa-
tion of the same aero-
plane (a Bf 109G) to
the model scales most
commonly used.*

A Kingcobra in 1/72 scale from the French firm H. incorporates photo-engraved small parts for inter detailing. Below: A striking model of a Vought F Cutlass.

s Ju 87B Stuka in 1/32 scale. A model of impressive proportions ideal for meticulous detailing.

Messerschmitt Bf 109E. A Hasegawa kit in 1/48 scale, this example has been finished in Spanish Civil War colours.

An ideal complement to this kit is a Verlinden conversion set, intended for superdetailing the interior and engine using photoetch and resin parts.

EVOLUTION OF THE SCALES

Despite the advantages of 1/72 scale it will soon be realised that much of the detail work done does not stand out well. If the modeller's interest is primarily detailing and careful painting, with less emphasis on quantity, the ideal size is therefore 1/48. This scale has recently seen renewed interest by manufacturers and many superb kits have appeared on the market.

A more considered step by the novice modeller is to tackle models in 1/32 scale. In this scale the range of subjects is noticeably reduced – single-seat fighters and some twins predominate.

But in choosing a large scale model the individual can do as much work as desired with a final option perhaps of motorising the kit.

Even larger are the aeroplane kits to 1/24 scale. Within the field of miniatures it is relatively uncommon; some of the available models have disappeared from catalogues although the size has intrinsic value in that a vast amount of superdetailing can be carried out, including adding practically everything the real aircraft can carry.

*The Messerschmitt Bf 109 is without doubt, the one aircraft that manufactures and modellers have seemingly endless fascinati***
In this case the kit is an Airfix Bf 109F in 1/48 scale.

Typical Luftwaffe tropical camouflage of sand, green and blue carefully applied with an airbrush. Note the careful paint blending and attractive overall finish.

The cockpit interior has been improved by reducing the ness of the seat and pilot's protective headrest. The Gru badge appropriate to this aircraft was specially made.

TOWARDS PERFECT REPRODUCTIONS

Until a few years ago 1/24 scale was the largest scale for plastic model aircraft but in the last decade the Japanese manufacturer Hasegawa launched a Museum Series - aeroplanes to 1/8 and 1/6 scales. These perfect reproductions of their respective subjects are limited to aircraft of the First World War and the Wright Flyer I. Kit materials are mixed and include plastic, wood and metal components.

From these giant scales, one can go to the exceedingly small models in 1/100, 1/144 and 1/200 scales. The aeroplane kits in these sizes obviously have less detail but they are useful for dioramas of air bases, or models of aircraft carriers. There are few enthusiasts who make such models with aims other than those mentioned.

AIRCRAFT MODELLING POSSIBILITIES

In can therefore be seen that an enormous spectrum opens up for the enthusiast aviation modeller who has both quantity and quality available to him from a huge selection of injection moulded plastic kits, all of which can be enhanced by a range of photo-engraved brass, resin and vacuum-formed additions, not to mention a great many alternative decals offering hundreds of colour schemes.

va's 1/32 scale Hellcat is a quality model with a multi-part engine. A realistic nish was been achieved with an airbrush and some hand painting.

XIX painted in the colours of Nationalist Spain. A vacuum-formed kit, duced by Vacukit in 1/48 scale.

us del Gran Poder', another Breguet XIX with ve fuselage markings.

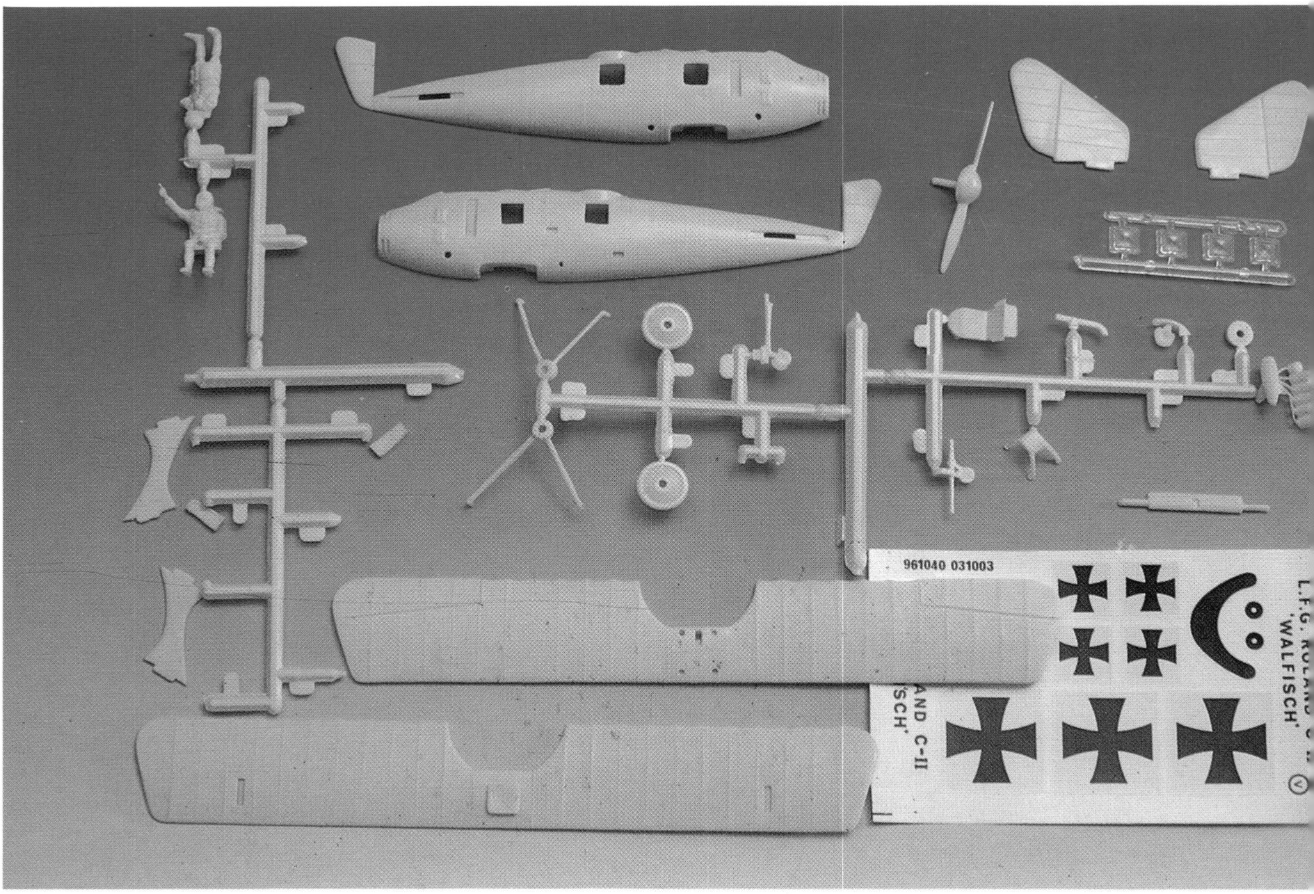

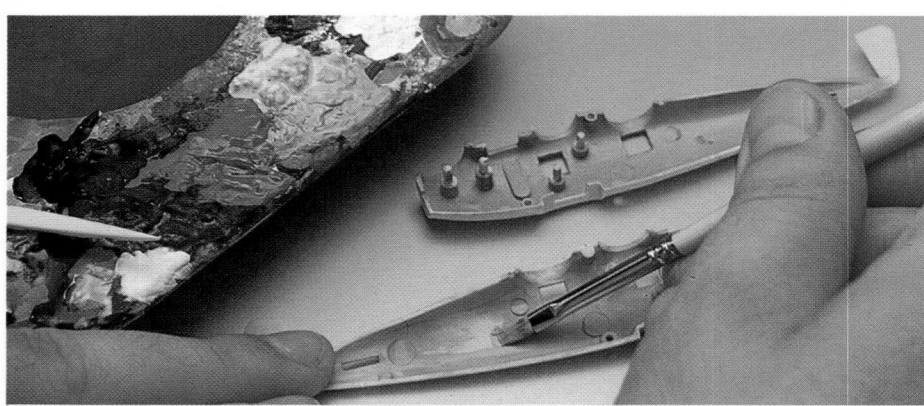

replica. Any model from this
aviation – in any scale – will
similar demands on the builder's
A model can be built 'straigh
the box' but by adding deta
finished result can be much imp

Basic construction will be c
first; later the painting proc
explained, along with the tech
used. We have already cho
brighter colour scheme tha
suggested by the manufacture
that we feel better matche
Roland's aesthetic appeal.

Roland C.II in 1/72 scale

First World War aeroplanes, with
their relative simplicity, make
particularly attractive models.
Although their assembly does not
involve any special difficulties, the
final rigging of any biplane can be a
challenge. In this first part of the
building process we will analyse
construction, making minor improve-
ments to the basic kit along the way.
The Roland is a good subject as it
encompasses all the problems likely to
be encountered in building a biplane

Once the compo-
nents are detached
from the sprue, the
first job is to paint
the cockpit interior
a medium brown
shade.

Both front fuselage
halves are finished
in black after the
engine is painted.

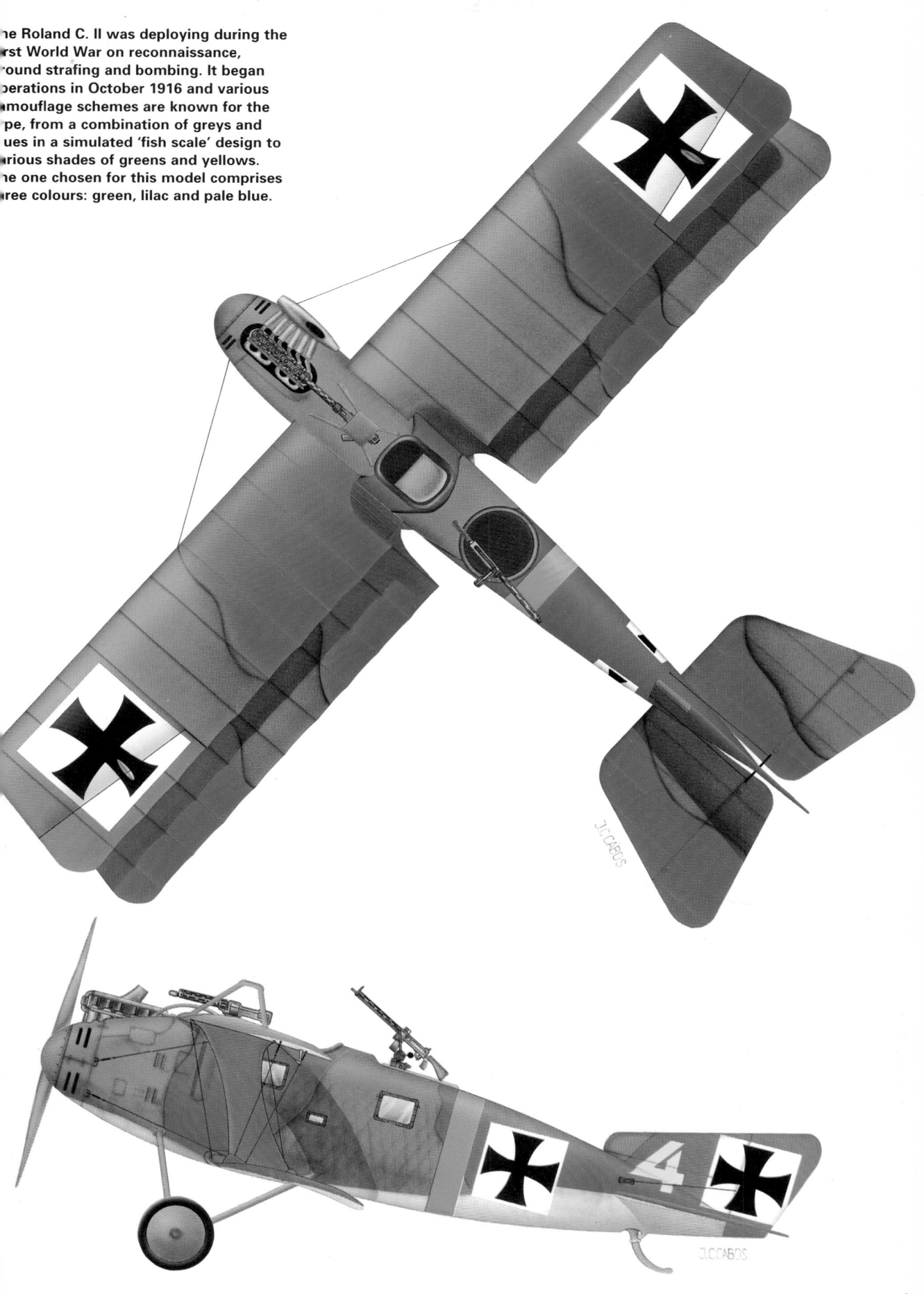

The Roland C. II was deploying during the First World War on reconnaissance, ground strafing and bombing. It began operations in October 1916 and various camouflage schemes are known for the type, from a combination of greys and blues in a simulated 'fish scale' design to various shades of greens and yellows. The one chosen for this model comprises three colours: green, lilac and pale blue.

9

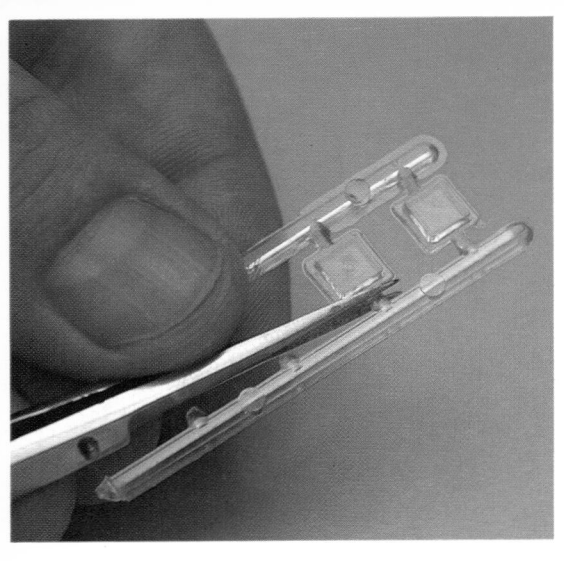

The plastic used for the clear parts is very brittle and it requires carefully separating from the sprue by making a clean cut with sharp scissors or a scalpel. The windows are glued into the fuselage with cyanoacrylate. Rolands had small 'curtains' at the windows and thin card or foil can be used to simulate them.

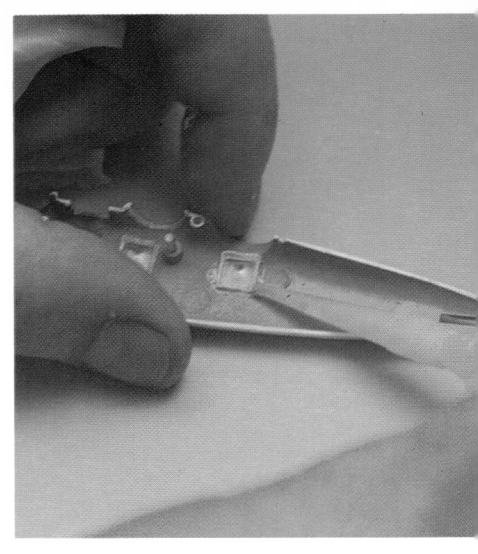

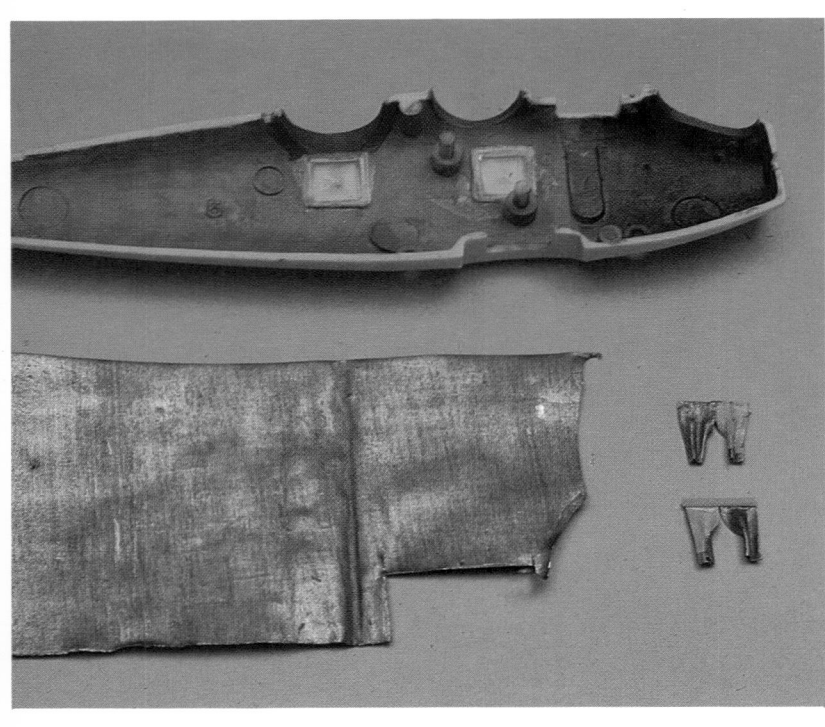

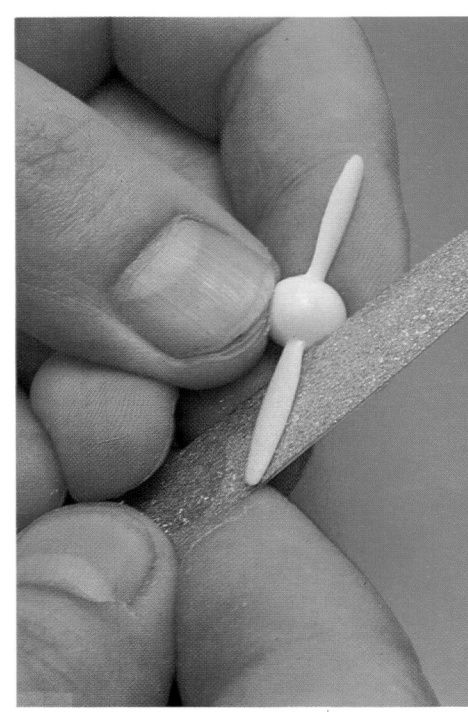

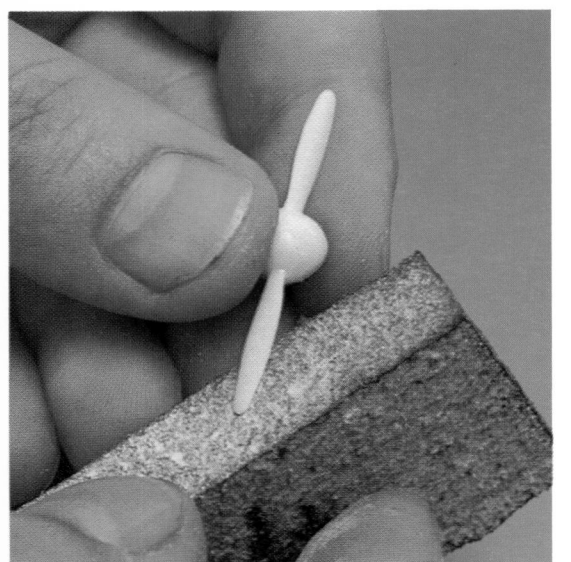

The propeller is thick and rather crudely reproduced, so reshape to obtain a cleaner aerodynamic shape.

Final finishing with fine grade 'wet and dry' sandpaper attached to a flexible backing block.

Wing struts are treated in the same way, using a half-round file which follows the contours quite easily.

NE DETAILING

...oland C.II had a 160 hp Mercedes ...n engine which is represented ...crudely in the kit. Immediate ...vement will be apparent by ...small details using copper wire ...erent thicknesses. The exhaust ...cylinders, rocker arms and so ...an all be represented with wire. ...located, these 'extras' are ...black with the engine block ...out in aluminium using the dry ...technique. The exhaust pipes ...bulky silencer which looks real- ...hen painted with a mixture of ...and brown applied with a dry

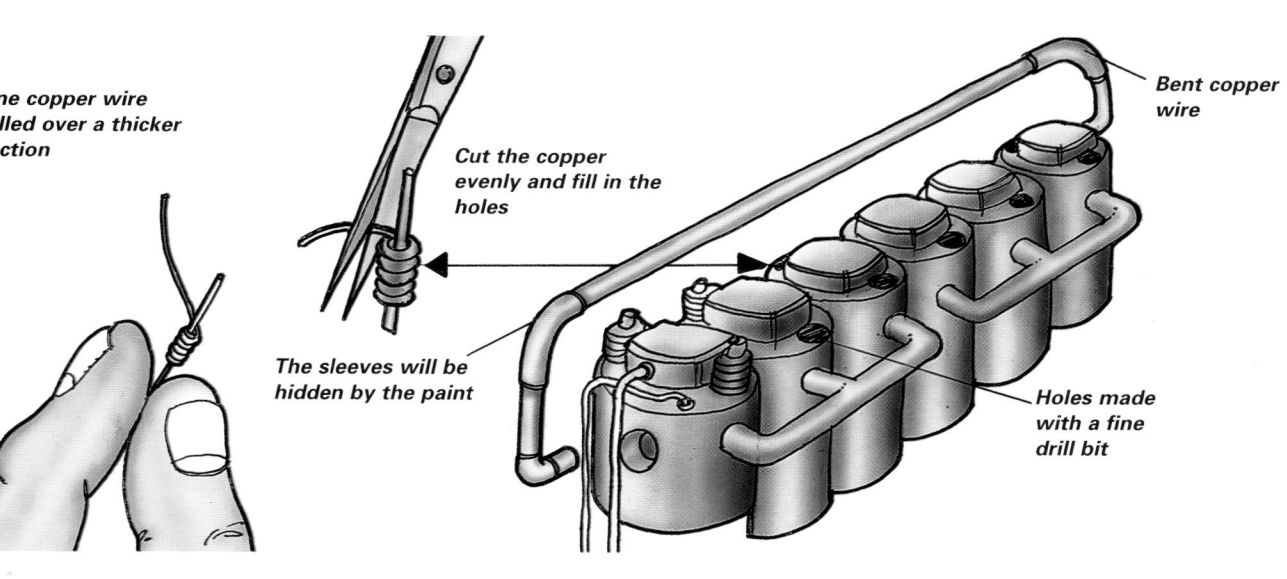

*...ne copper wire
...lled over a thicker
...ction*

*Cut the copper
evenly and fill in the
holes*

*Bent copper
wire*

*The sleeves will be
hidden by the paint*

*Holes made
with a fine
drill bit*

KEY MATERIALS

*Use of body putty
is often necessary
to achieve invis-
ible joints.*

*Some putties are
dissolved in
acetone and a
double container is
useful when
applying these.*

*A putty or palette
knife is used for
filling the larger
gaps whereas a
brush is adequate
for smaller ones.*

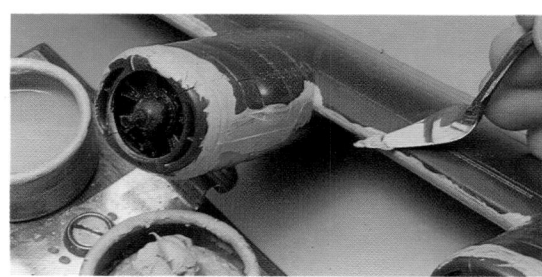

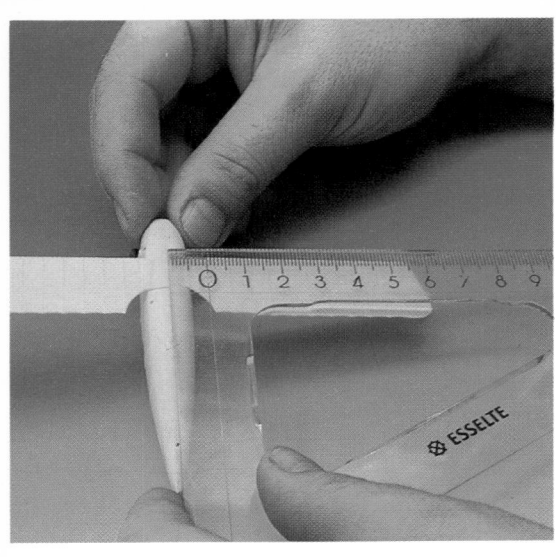

Join the fuselage halves and glue the lower wing sections together, checking correct alignment with a set square.

Using putty, every gap or seam can be sealed.

Once the putty has dried all surfaces are lightly sanded.

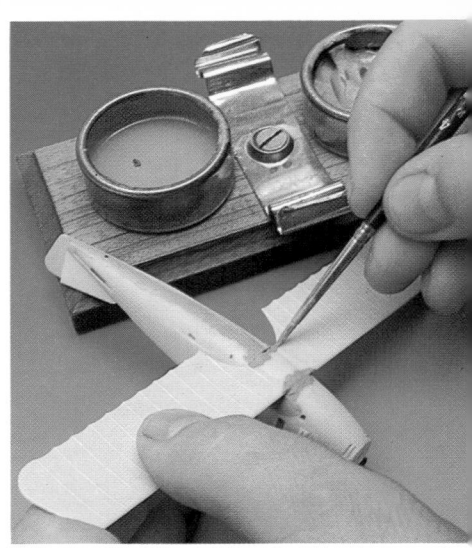

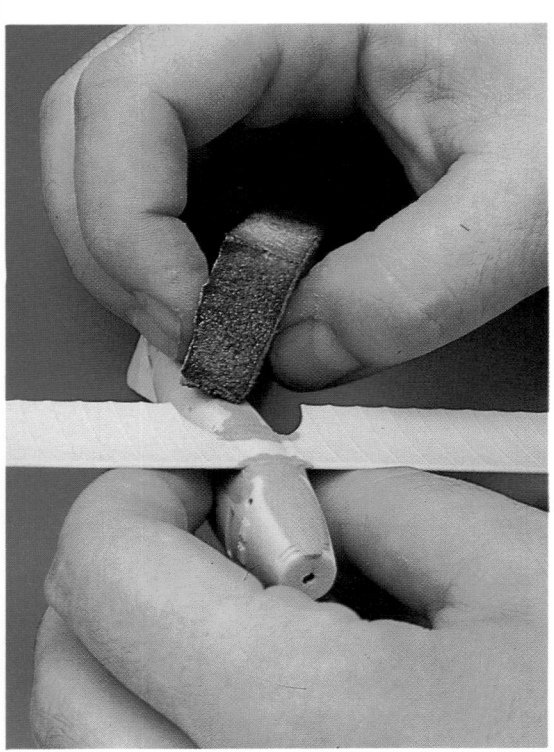

The uppper wing sections are glued together, again checking alignment.

When making frames for the fuse-lage windows, a small calibrator is useful.

The dimensions are traced onto fine (0.2mm) plastic card.

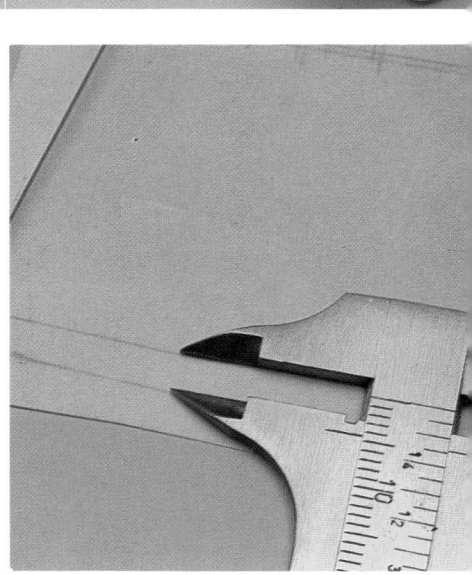

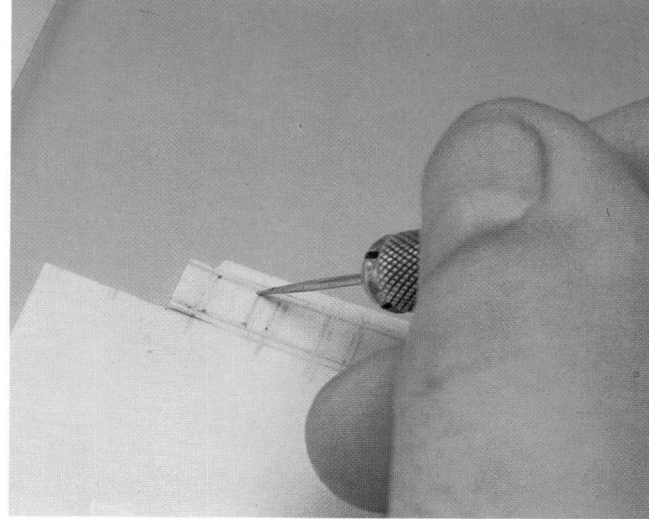

DETAILS

...g some small additional ... in this case window ...nds and mainwheel covers, is ...fficult. Very thin plastic is ...d and if this is not available ...pecialist hobby shops, it is ...ly easy to adapt domestic ... packaging such as detergent ...ers.

Using a pencil and rule, draw parallel lines the size of the window frames.

Mark the corners to be cut with a punch.

For a clean cut, use a small steel rule and a sharp modelling knife or scalpel.

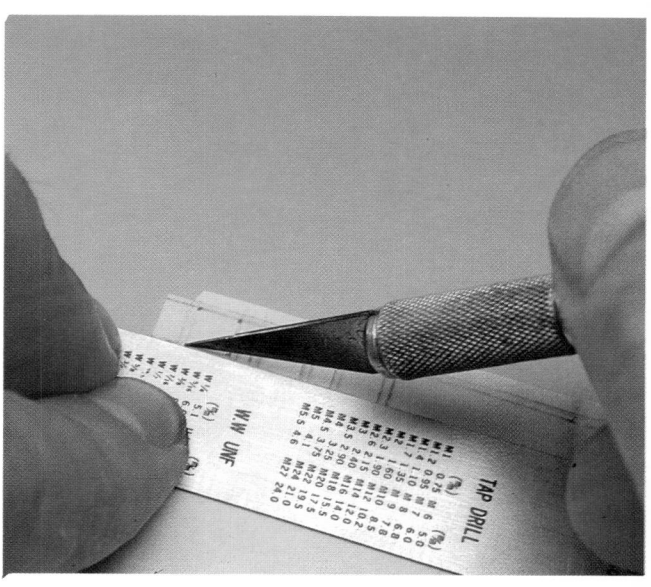

DETAILS ADDED TO THE MODEL

Cooling collector

Piston rings

Oil cooler

The entire front section of the fin and its supports

Windscreen

Fastening cable on ammunition drum

Window frame

Small curtain

Wheel cover

All airframe bracing wires

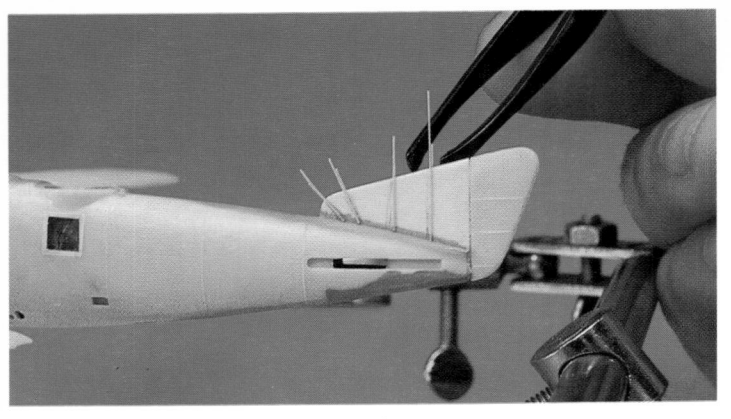

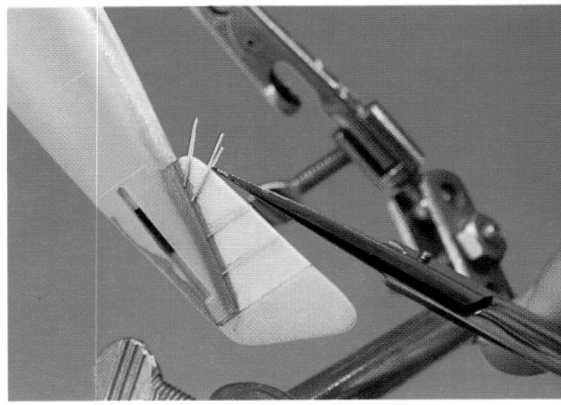

The fin in the kit is inaccurate and in order to correct it the orginal has to be cut away from the fuselage and replaced, new wire braces being made from very thin plastic strip. All excess plastic was finally removed with fine scissors. Once the wing struts are in place, the model is finished and ready for painting.

APPLYING THREE COLOUR CAMOUFLAGE

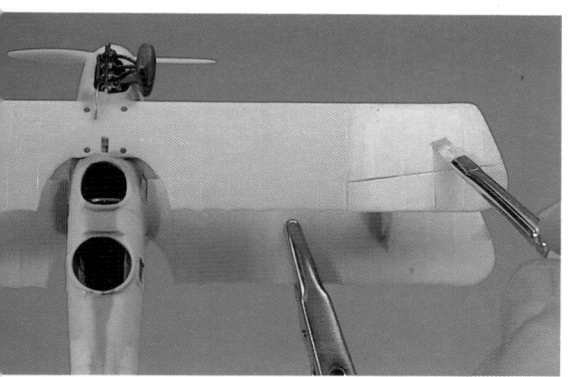

Wing areas where the black crosses will be applied are painted white rather than using decals.

Masking procedure

Although the kit includes decals, we preferred to paint some areas, particularly the square ground for the crosses.

The first step is to paint the white squares on wings and fuselage and then prepare masks using transparent adhesive masking film of the type supplied for airbrush painting. If this material is not to hand, masks can be made up with several layers

TING A ROLAND IN 2 SCALE

ishing this model, all types of t application have been loyed. In conjunction with painting, self-adhesive g masks were used for als and the insignia and the f colour on the fuselage was ted with Letraline. Maskol used to cover the small vs while painting proceeded olour film paints.

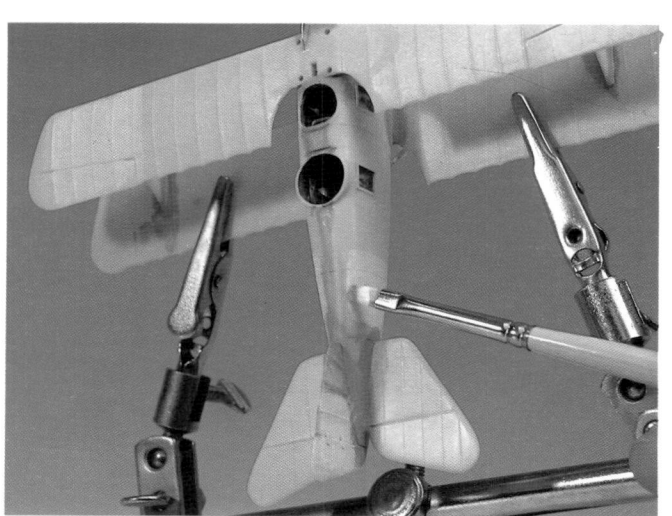

Similar treatment for the fuselage insignia locations. It is better to paint relatively large areas even if decals are provided as the latter are prone to cracking and lifting, particularly if they are thick. Commercial products designed to soften decal film largely overcomes this problem, however.

It is not nece
to outline the
patch as the
sions will be
defined by th
colour.

Taking the measurements, draw and cut squares on the transparent masking tape or ordinary masking tape with its adhesion reduced.

Apply the mask to blank off each square.

Mixing blue and red creates the lilac shade that forms part of the camouflage pattern.

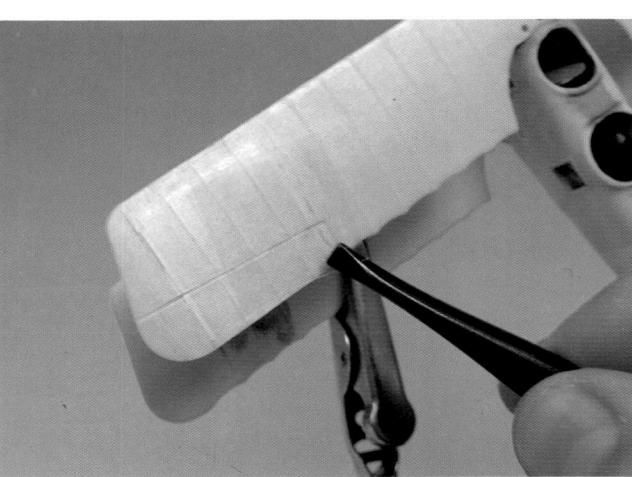

of transparent masking tape stuck together and cut to size.

As some self-adhesive paper is strong enough to lift paint, it needs rubbing between the fingers to reduce stickiness. Masking tape has just the right amount of adhesion but some pressure is usually needed to prevent paint creeping under the edges.

Our first camouflage colour is blue-lilac, obtained by mixing a strong blue and a little bright red. The paint is thinned to ensure that no brush marks are visible. A No 3 flat brush and a No 2 round brush are used, the latter for blending the

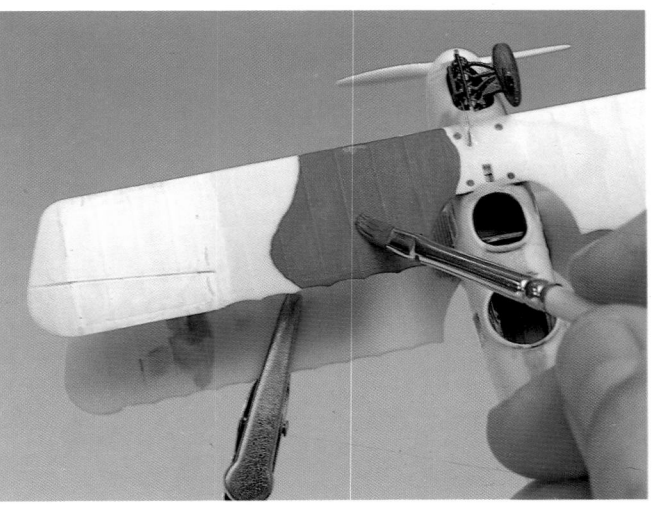

Flat brushes
ideal for larg
and contours
be followed
pointed brus.
applying a fi
coat with a f
brush.

The windows are covered with Maskol liquid mask.

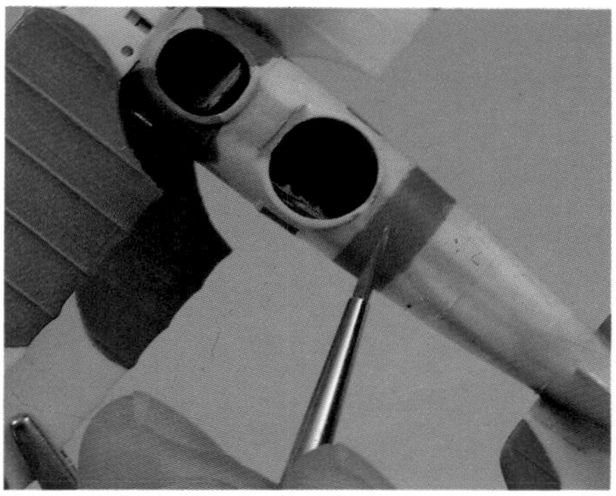

At this stage the red fuselage band is painted without worrying about the outlines.

The red band is subsequently masked with flexible tape.

1

2

3

4

5

range of colours, thinnned down for application with a dry brush:
purple 2: Medium purple 3: Dark green 4: Medium green 5: Red (for the band)

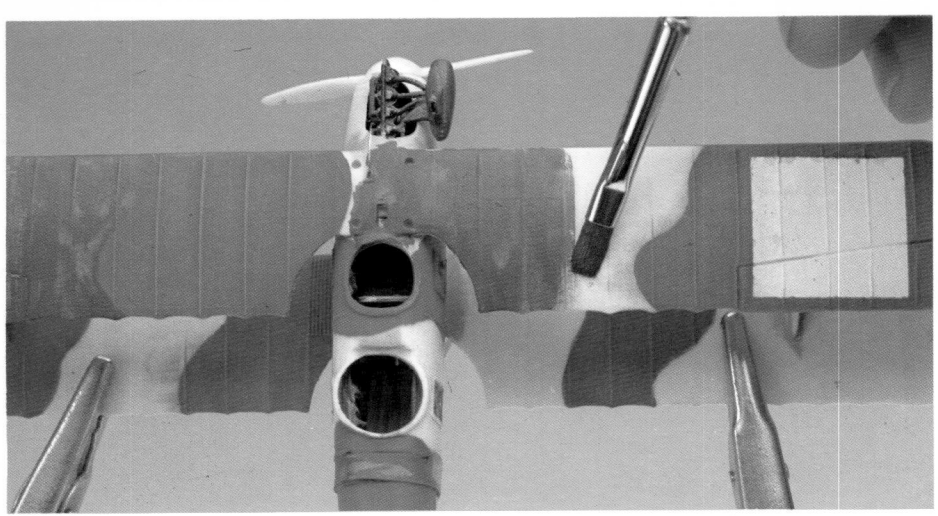

The green used is a mixture [...]
green with a little black. It is [...]
as previously although at th[...]
more care should be taken [...]
the edges of the two colours [...]
avoid a thick build-up of pain[...]
the demarkation lines.

Painting the propeller

Green is also applied to the p[...]
spinner; the blades themselve[...]
to have the effect of lam[...]
wood.

A base coat of light br[...]
applied to the entire blade are[...]
brown sienna, lines are m[...]
indicate the first layer of [...]
taking care to keep them uni[...]

Painting on the green colour, starting with a slightly darker mix than the final coat. Two coats will be necessary for good coverage.

A base coat of medium brown is applied to the propeller blades to simulate wood.

Dark brown is used to indicate the plywood composite of the real propeller.

A darker brown enables a wood [...] effect to be achieved.

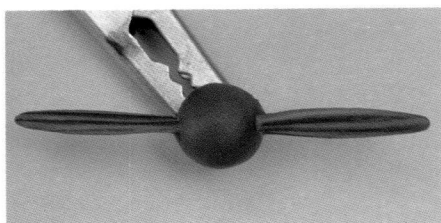

As a finishing touch, clear varnish is applied to the propeller blades.

edges of each colour. The model is held steady with articulated tweezers.

Paint is brushed on evenly without leaving marks, and applied in two thin layers which will allow surface detail to show through. The small windows are protected by Maskol before the fuselage is painted, the red band being painted freehand as this will be masked with tape when the green shade is applied.

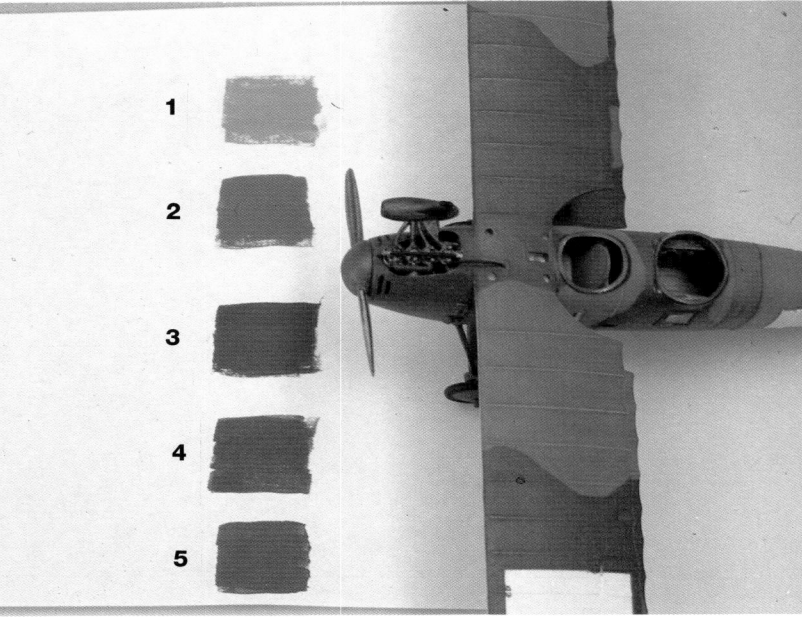

In order to achieve a realistic reproduction of plywood, three or four colours w[...] needed: medium brown, dark brown (for the grain), very dark brown (also for t[...] grain) green camouflage and finally a green for dry-brushing.

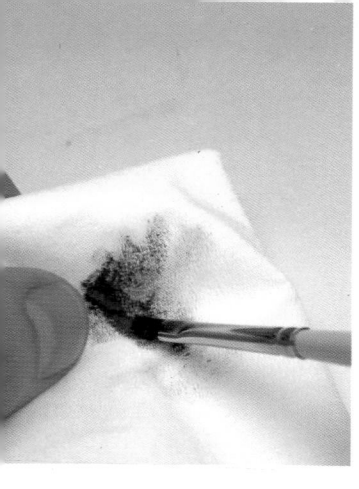

Discharge of paint over a cloth or paper in preparation for dry brushing.

With very little paint on the brush, the surface is rubbed over quickly and lightly.

ze propeller blades were
made from laminated strips
od. The next colour, a dark
brown, is partially superim-
on the lighter shade. Finally, a
colour is used for outlining
blade.

rush

echnique, widely used on
of tanks and vehicles, can
hance the texture of fabric

Dry brushing with the contrasting lighter colours uses the same technique.

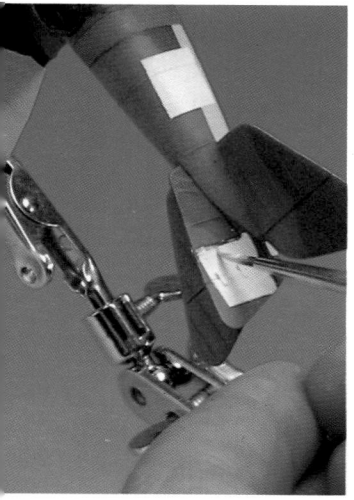

reas behind the crosses are now
ed to straighten the edges.

s and the shape of the ribs of
aircraft. Using a very soft
nd rubbing with the fingers
ally be sufficient, although a
uch is necessary to ensure
effect looks realistic.
each base colour a corre-
ng lighter shade is
ed: from olive green mixed
ack to pure green thinned to

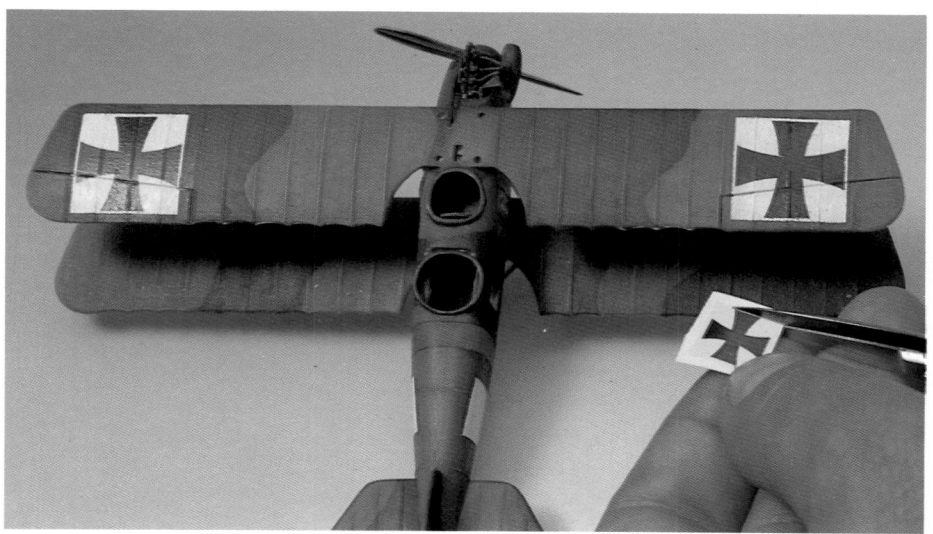

Using pointed scissors, the decal images are cut as close as possible to ensure that no transparent film remains.

The white rudder square,
its confluence with the fusel...
better painted with a brush.
to use templates in this area
invariably involve some retou...
Before applying the decal o...
these are carefully cut aroun...
placed on their white square...
Micro Set and Micro Sol to...
them pliable and allow th...
'flow' over the rib contours.

The aircraft number '4' is...
separately on paper, cut out t...
a template and painted on...
brush. Care is needed when...
off the mask as some pain...
creep under the edges, neces...
retouching – indeed this...
common problem when...
masks as their edges tend to...
in places. It is advisable to...
supply of matching paint to...
retouching proves to be nece...

The number is drawn on a piece of paper, transferred onto a self-adhesive mask and cut out. It is then placed on the model ready for painting.

A hole is made in the wing surface to take the bracing wire supports. The hole is widened slightly in order to insert a piece of plasticard which is glued and cut.

an almost clear wash. Letting paint dry on the brush so that the bristles hardly move enables dry brushing to proceed on flying surfaces. Little by little the fabric and ribs appear in relief, highlighted by the almost dry paint.

A similar procedure is followed for the lilac colour and the lower surfaces, which are finished in a very pale blue. To bring out some of the inevitable wear and tear of a front line aircraft, a very soft ochre water colour wash can be applied with final dry brushing using white slightly tinted with brown.

g bracing
constitutes
nal, special
that sets
e models
A number of
ine strands of
ed plastic
will be
ed and it is a
dea to make
han needed
e of breakage.

millimetres. On the wings, location of the bracing wires is most convenient when working from the fuselage outwards.

To secure each wire a small area of paint is scraped off using a modelling knife and a small drop of cyanoacrylate is applied to the end of the wire to secure it to the paint-free area. Once this has set the total length of the wire can be determined and cut as necessary. It is important to keep the wire taut and not allow it to bend. This operation is repeated where the wire is to be secured at

The logical way to position bracing wires is from inside to outside. The strips are glued by cyanoacrylate at one end, allowing for a little extra length for trimming at the other end.

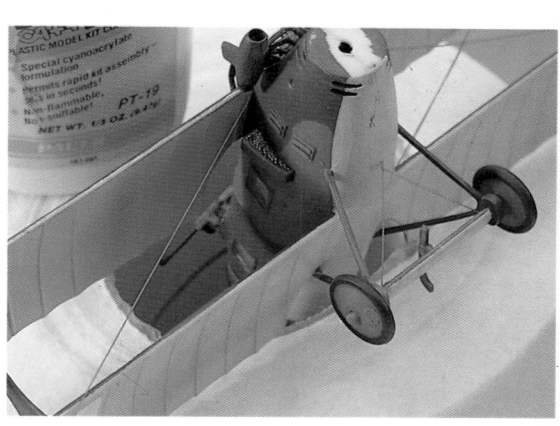

ng wires

sential detail on models of World War aeroplanes is to ring, tailplane and undercarbracing wires under the tion tension. Although s types of wire and sewing s have been used in the past, est results are obtained by hin strips of heat-stretched , usually made from the which carry the main compoparts. When strips of sufficient ave been made these are red with a calibrator or rule immed to the required length, ng an extra three or four

Once the right length is obtained, the wires are cut and glued.

the other end, the drop of cyanoacrylate being most easily applied with the aid of a toothpick or similar tool rather than directly from the tube or tin. This can be a delicate operation, but with practice excellent results can be achieved.

The joint will be somewhat obvious so it needs painting over with the tip of a fine brush. Varnishing the model will also ensure that the bracing wires stay tight.

FIRST STEPS IN MODELLING

ASSEMBLY OF A MiG-29

Having invariably spoilt a few cheap kits we move on to build our first 'quality' model. It is better to choose a kit that presents the least problems so look for a subject that has easy assembly of parts and good surface detail such as the Hasegawa MiG-29 Fulcrum in 1/72 scale.

In addition to its ease of assembly this kit has clear instructions, a choice of camouflage schemes and a comprehensive decal sheet. Because the cockpit has to be painted before the fuselage halves are joined, we recommend starting with the interior using enamel or gouache paints.

AIRBRUSHES IN ACTION

Airbrushes are precision instruments capable of remarkable finishes and effects but the beginner needs practice to develop a technique.

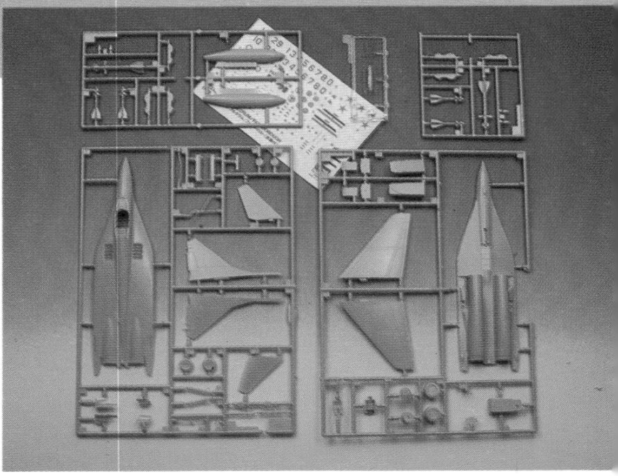

Kit parts that make up a modern Russian jet fighter exemplified by the Hasegawa MiG-29 Fulcrum in 1/72 scale. The component mouldings are excellent and there is no complex assembly work.

The first step is to paint the cockpit and pilot figure with acrylic gouache which mixes well and has good covering properties.

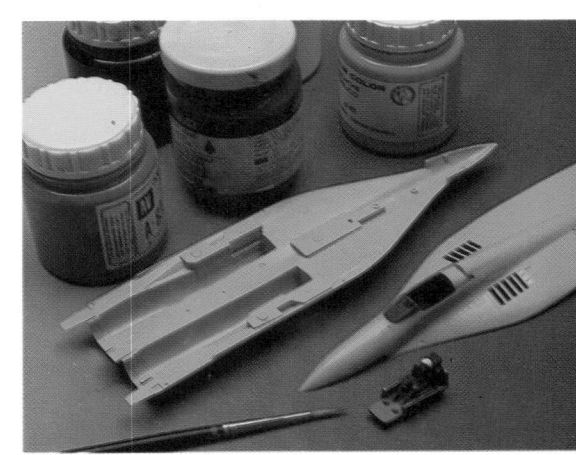

KEY MATERIALS

Other important modelling tools include flexible sandpaper blocks. These foam rubber pads come with the abrasive material attached in the form of a different grade of sandpaper on each side. Two types are available, giving a total of four different grades of paper. Dry body putty is easily rubbed down using a flexible sanding block as it adapts easily to curves. For a final polish of filled areas, a sponge pan scourer is ideal.

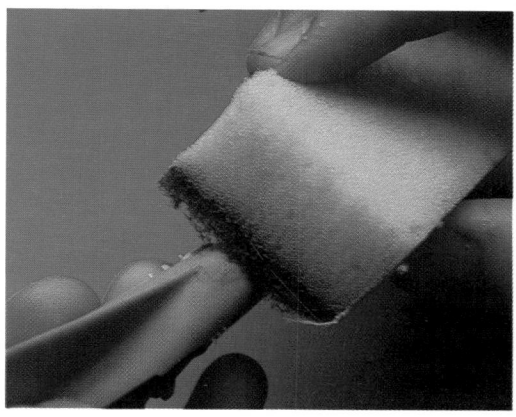

On this kit the only areas that require filling are minute sink marks on the wings and rudders.

Putty has to be applied both above and below the wing.

Paint the pilot's flying suit in deep blue, using a small amount of white to bring out creases, pockets and so on.

Before applying the instrument panel decal, the cockpit interior is painted black and finished in medium grey using a dry brush.

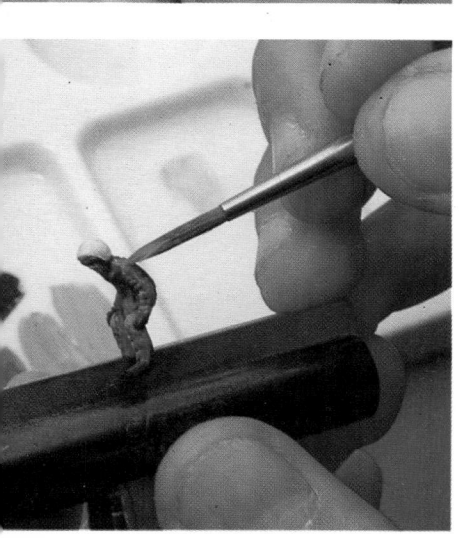

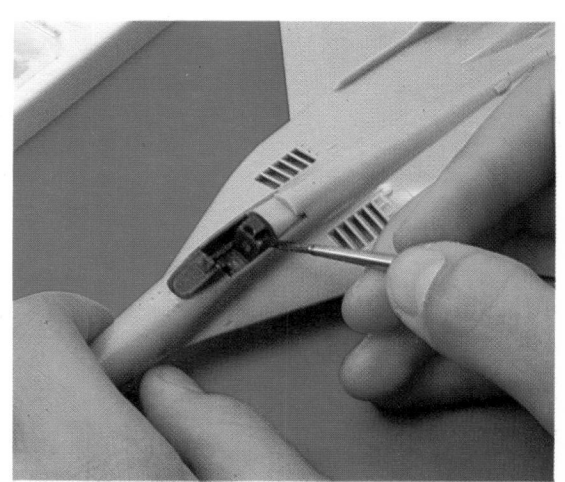

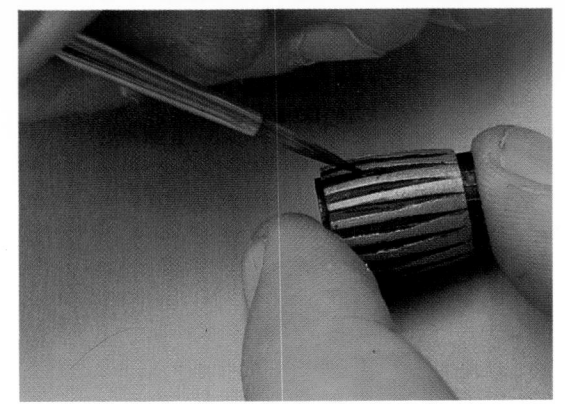

The jet nozzl
require a spe
treatment: af
they are high
in black, a m
silver, brown
black is appli
using the dry
technique.

An airbrush represents a considerable investment and it requires great care both in use and maintenance if we want it to last.

To obtain good airbrush performance a reliable supply of air is essential. A compressor is by far the best but good painting results can be obtained with individual canisters of air. With airbrush and propellant to hand the right paint solution is vital. In general paint will flow well through an airbrush if it has the consistency of milk and this is the procedure followed to paint our MiG-29.

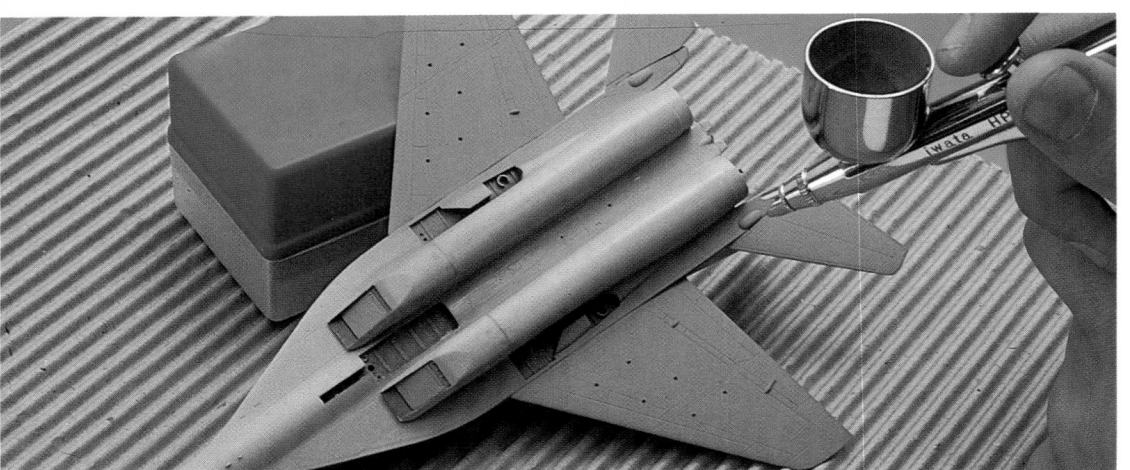

The result is
metallic effec
gives the
convincing a
ance of heate
metal.

The best way
paint a mode
modern aero
is with an air
Start with lig
colours, in th
a soft grey.

Don't forget
mask the fini
cockpit area
spraying.

Cockpit mask
with masking
and tissue pa

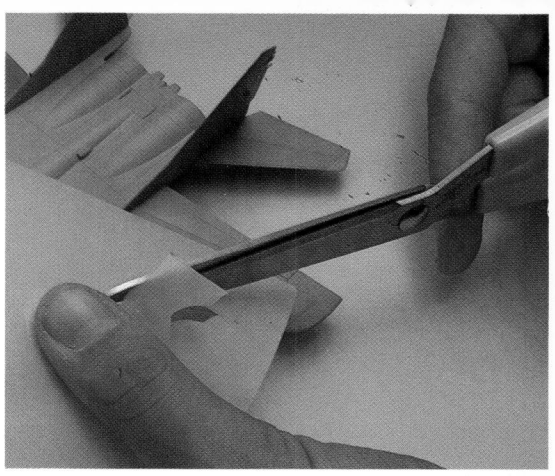

Before applying the second colour, outlines of the camouflage pattern are drawn on translucent paper.

Cut out the shapes, leaving only the area to be painted. Hold the paper mask steady.

To obtain soft edges it is sufficient to hold the mask 1-2mm away from the model surface.

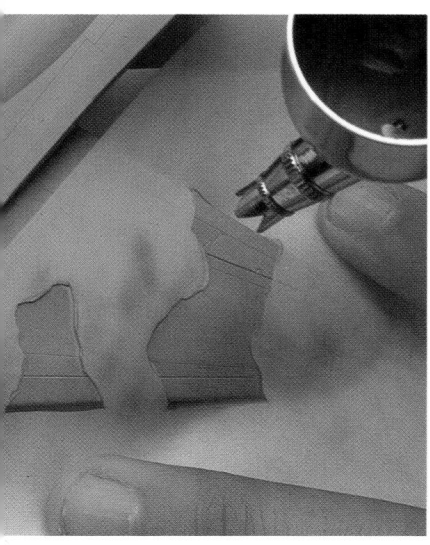

We used acylic paints on the MiG, these having the advantage of being soluble in water. Brushes can be more thoughly cleaned in alcohol which is quite cheap to buy.

Each airbrush had different characteristics but ideally the one chosen for modelling purposes should be capable of spraying a variety of line thicknesses from about 0.05 mm to 8 or 10mm wide. A versatile airbrush will enable large areas as well as fine lines to be sprayed quickly.

If you have a steady hand, patches and other small areas can be painted freehand; grip the wrist of the brush hand in the other to improve steadiness. Don't worry if you tremble and make a ragged line, as raised or elevated masks can be used to cover any mistakes by going over a particular area a second time. In hand-painting as well as airbrushing, the rule of light colours first applies. Clean the airbrush thoroughly after every painting session.

To prevent the acrylic finish wearing or being scratched, it is

craft's anti-
anel is
black using
and brush.

e decals
and just
they come
ely free of
cking paper,
them on
del in the
locations
ng to the
tions.

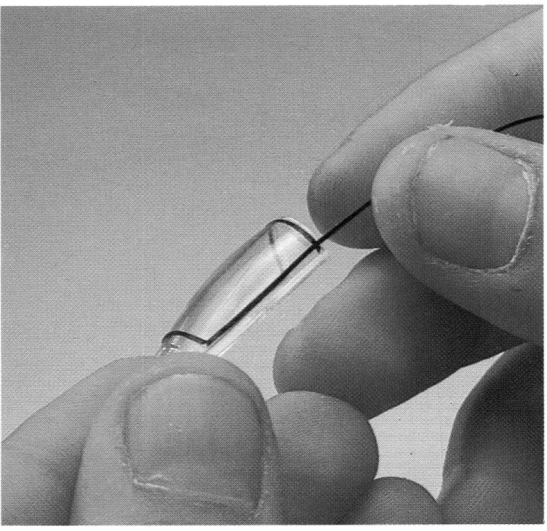

This model includes a large number of small decals.

Some decals are positioned with the aid of small tweezers.

In order to paint the cockpit framing it must first be masked with tape.

Maskol is applied to all transparent areas prior to painting.

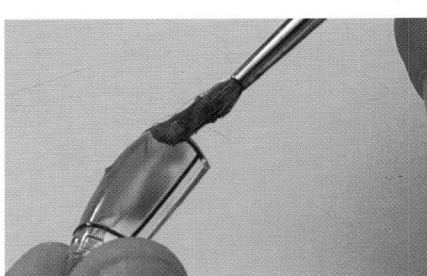

BEGINNERS' MISTAKES

The completed MiG-29 is compared with a Mirage made by the same individual when he lacked modelling experience. On a close comparison some important points emerge.

Analysis of the mistakes made by the beginner:

Obvious gaps and seams where parts have been joined reveal that no filler has been used.

Shiny decals contrast with matt paintwork due to not varnishing the model to obtain uniformity.

Cockpit framing badly painted, or not painted at all.

Badly applied paint has led to some variation of camouflage colour.

Made up colours due to a of reference material.

Only the external stores remain to be painted and placed on their appropriate pylons.

The finished MiG-29 looks very impressive, well representing the current high 'state of the art' regarding quality of plastic kit moulding.

advisable to apply a coat of gloss varnish. Decals adhere better to a gloss surface with their own gloss finish blending in well, but a final coat of satin finish varnish gives a better look to a high-performance jet fighter. A bonus is that a varnished model will never lose its decals and neither will sunlight fade or yellow these with the passing of time.

The foregoing procedure is that followed by a 13-year old model maker, so large numbers of modellers will be equally able to complete kits to this standard. There are however, many methods and 'tricks of the trade' to improve the process and these will be explained throughout the following chapters.

STEP BY STEP CONSTRUCTION

*Filling indentations
between the
fuslage and
rudders with putty.*

*The wing joint has
to be sealed and
sandpapered.*

*Use a scribe and
punch to restore
any rivet and panel
line detail that may
be erased when
rubbing down.*

After carefully constructi
model, the final touch is
any gaps in the sub-asse
with putty and rub down thoro
It is often the case that wing t
lage joints, tailplane junction
ings and so on will not mate e
so a body putty treatment is
sary for a smooth finish. Ma
the application of putty us
brush and acetone will
pleasing results with no
seam lines or gaps. Bear in
that putty tends to shrink
drying and a second appli

may be required. Alternatively a generous amount with some over-spill will do the job, the excess being rubbed down with fine, No 600 grade wet & dry sandpaper until every irregularity is smoothed over.

RECONSTRUCTION

It is not unusual to find when checking the component parts to make up a cockpit interior that although the manufucturer has provided some parts, others have been omitted. If the differences are only in detail, it may only be necessary to fabricate the missing items – but some kits provide only the barest of cockpit furnishings, leaving the modeller to build up instrument panels, consoles and seat detail from scratch. Plastic card in invaluable for making cockpits

Correcting design errors and omissions in kits can take time and effort but the end result is more than worthwhile. Extra detail such a control levers can be added by stretching plastic strip under a low heat in a match flame to create a small ball representing a control knob.

look more authentic, as is the stretched sprue method. Control detail can be added by drilling out a suitable recepticle, inserting a piece of card strip and gently heating this in the flame of a match. Under heating the plastic will form a small ball. Any number of these can be made to represent handgrips on control levers, these being drawn out to the required length.

Milling cutters can be used to drill out holes where necessary, reducing the thickness of the plastic incrementally. A hand drill is preferable as electric drills can soon become too hot and will melt the plastic. Drills with slow speed controls overcome this problem.

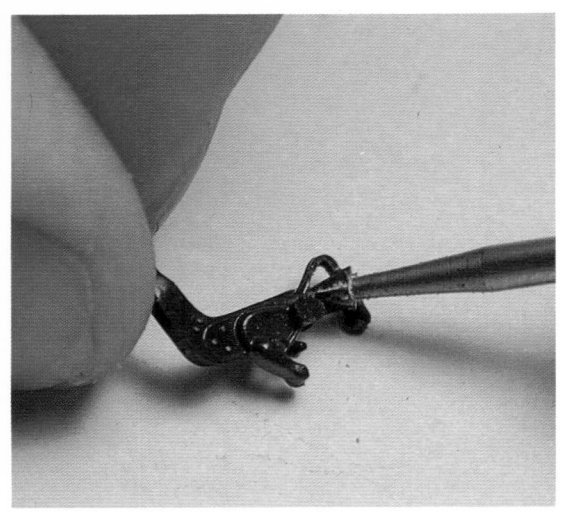

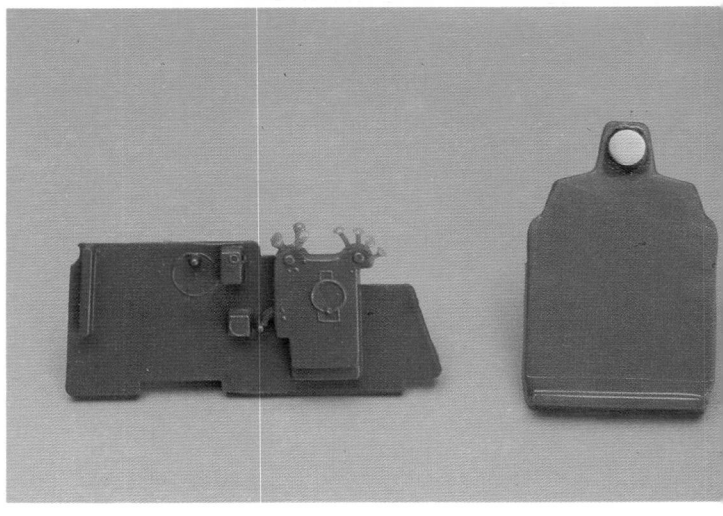

A milling cutter is used to hollow out controls that are moulded 'solid' in the kit.

The seat is improved by adding the headrest cushion.

Batteries and consoles are partially painted.

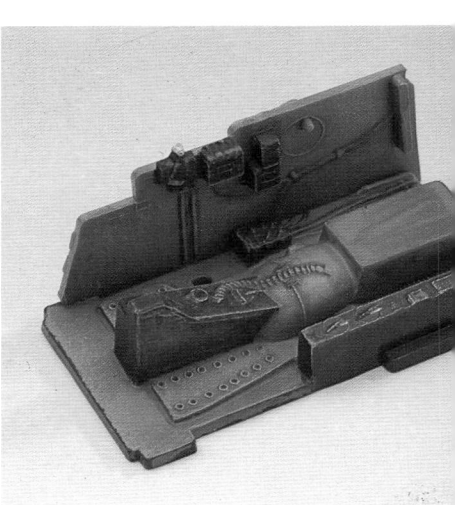

*Cockpit inte
sub-assemb
pre-painted
the dry brus
method.*

*note electric
wiring and c
lever additio
'used' look a
consoles.*

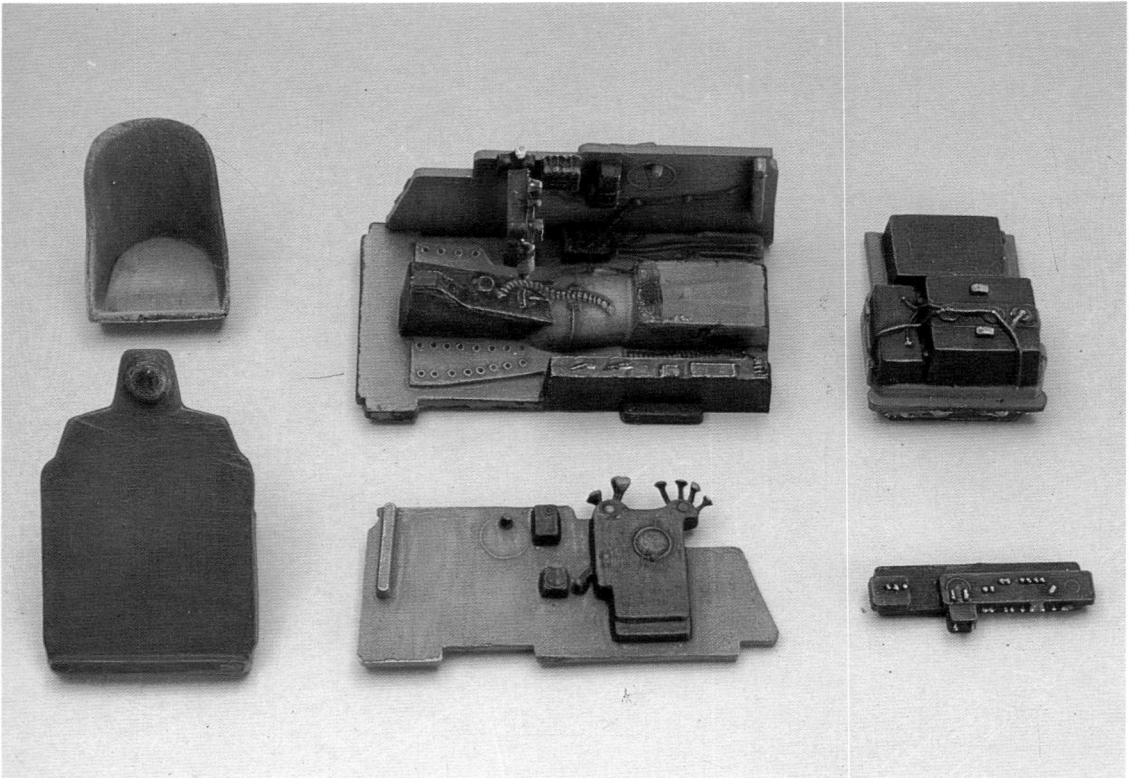

PAINTING THE INTERIOR

One of the unavoidable steps in the construction of an aeroplane kit is the painting of the interior. This means that all visible cockpit walls, wheel wells and fuselage areas where windows give an inside view must be coated in an apprpriate colour. In the case of this P-38 Lightning and other American aircraft of the Second World War period a special coating known as zinc chromate primerwas applied as an anti-corrosive. This had two distinct casts, yellow and green both being quite bright. Some modellers prefer to grey down zinc chromate so that it does not stand out although most primed areas of the model will be hidden by interior fittings. Dry brush again helps to give some effect of wear and to bring out detail on black-painted fittings.

On models of aircraft with tricycle landing gear there will invariably be a tendency for tail sitting. This is overcome by adding weight into the extreme nose or engine nacelles – if there is sufficient space.

tire interior
ed with anti-
ve primer, in
e with an
reen hue.

ve with an
tube is
r sticking
arriage
nents
r.

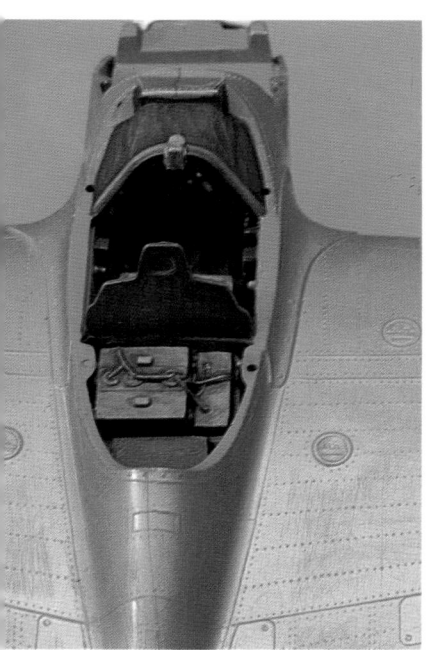

kpit interior and the instrument panel are painted matt black with an olive drab lower edge. As it is a tricycle gear aircraft, a
such as lead embedded in Plasticine is added to the nose to restore balance. The lead weights have to be well distributed
ulded' into the nose. Secure with putty if necessary.

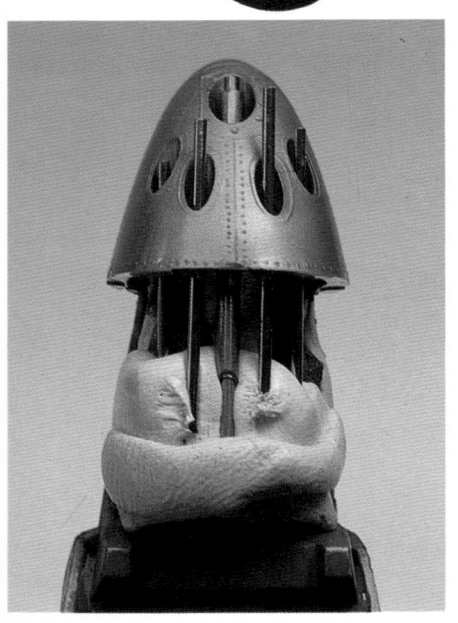

Machine guns and cannon supplied in the kit are subsituted by brass tubing and hypodermic needles held in place by epoxy putty.

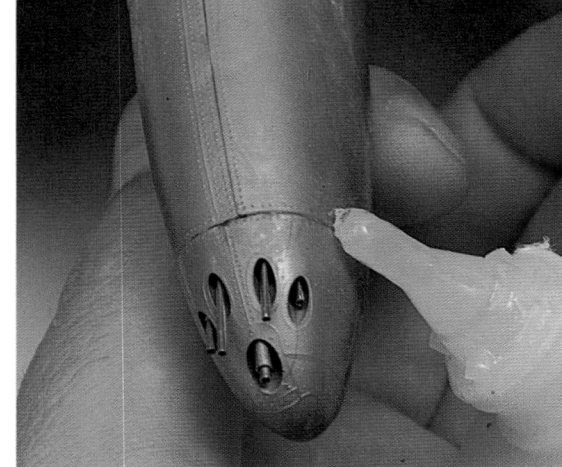

Modern cyanoacrylate adhesives are strong enough to use as putty.

Use of a cyanoacrylate hardening agent ensures immediate drying.

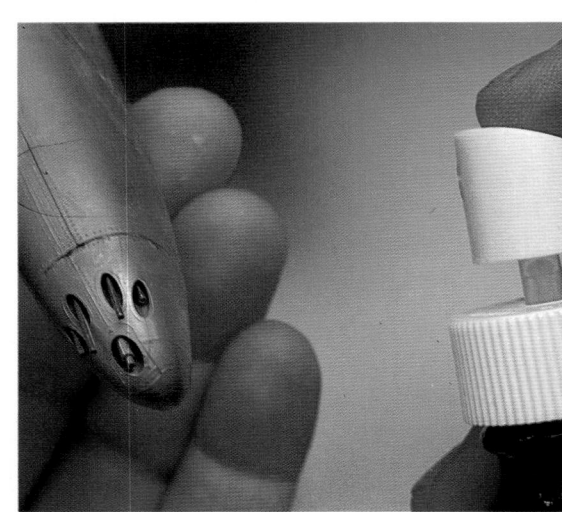

WEAPONS

Unless kit machine guns and cannon have very well mouded barrels these are best replaced by brass or plastic tubing. Hypodermic needles cut to length also make good gun barrels.

Hypodermic needles come in different thicknesses, some of which will be adaptable to 1/72 and 1/48 scale models. Shortening the needles may present a few prob-

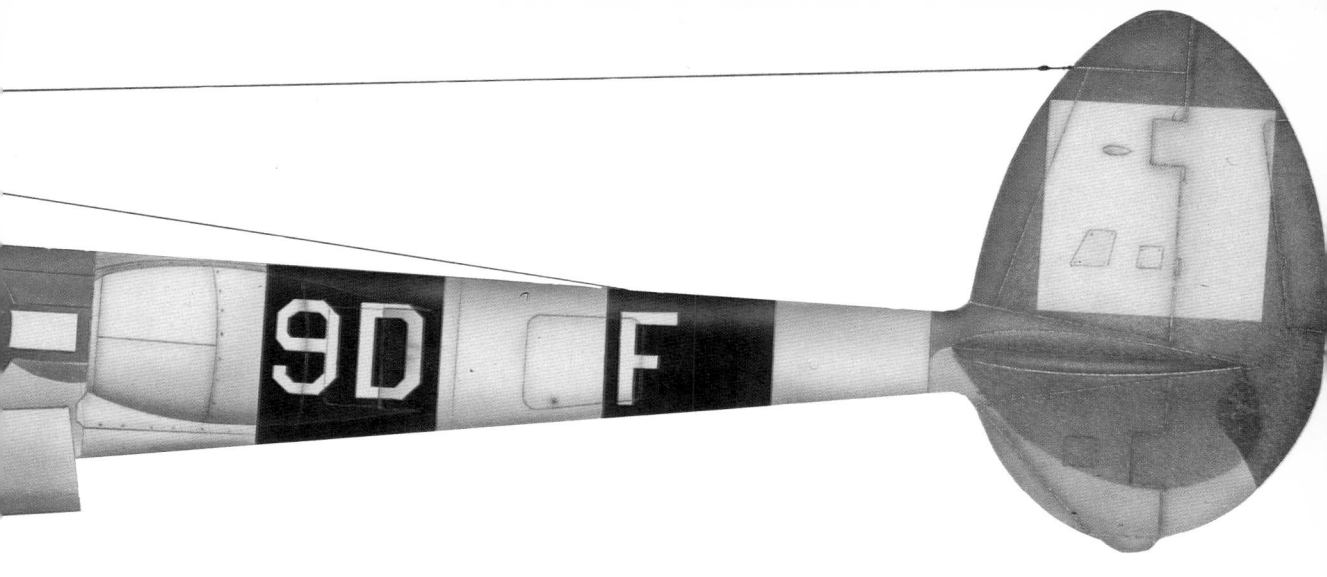

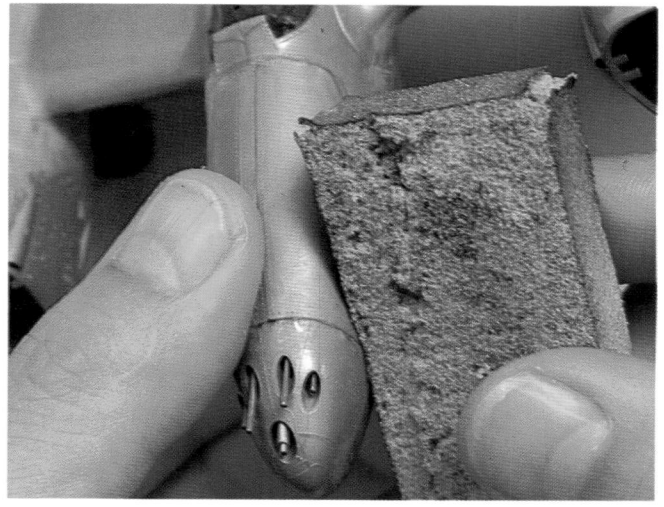

down an
panel with
dry sand-

ber to
rivet and
detail
sanding

lems although special cutting disks for just this purpose are supplied with mini drills. Alternatively, a triangular section watchmakers' file will enable the metal to be weakened enough to break it. Either procedure requires that the needles are held firmly in a vice and the clamp protected by small wooden wedges.

SECURING OPENING PANELS

On models that incorporate opening gun bay doors and hatches, affixing these in the closed position may reveal gaps. When glued in place careful use of sandpaper will help make them flush with the surrounding area.

If some gaps remain, these can be filled with putty or thick cyanoacrylate but if the latter is used a good hardening agent is essential. Quick drying adhesives such as these enable final rubbing down to be completed without delay. Loss of detail when rubbing down models in 1/72 scale is acceptable as this is often too heavy as moulded. Larger kits, to 1/48 scale and above, need to have rubbed away rivet and panel detail rescribed.

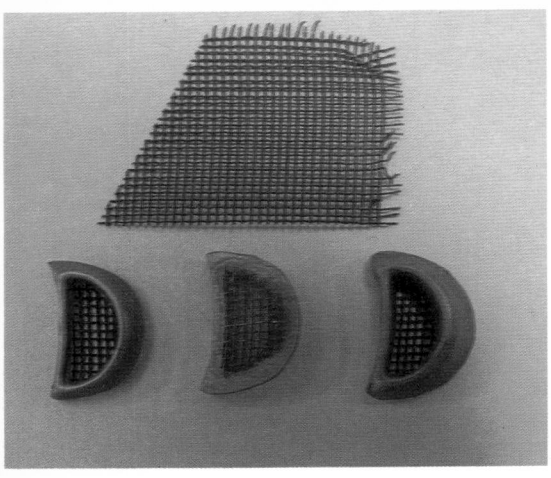

Air intake grilles help hide the fact that no engine is fitted - place the mesh inside before glueing.

Landing gear legs are enhanced by copper wire and paper clip sections representing braces and hydraulic brake lines. Both help strengthen landing gear oleos.

The rear end of each fuselage boom is hollow in the kit and both need blanking plates. First measure the width required.

An oval template comes in handy here as one will match the diameter of the P-38's tail-booms almost exactly.

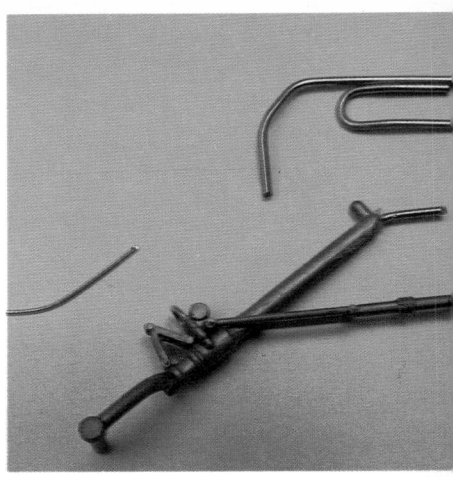

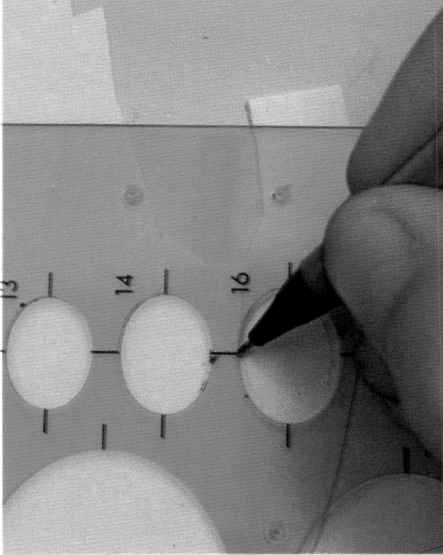

With fine scissors, cut the oval as neatly as possible out of plastic card. Sandpaper will improve the shape.

With the help of a square and punch, rivet and panel lines are scribed.

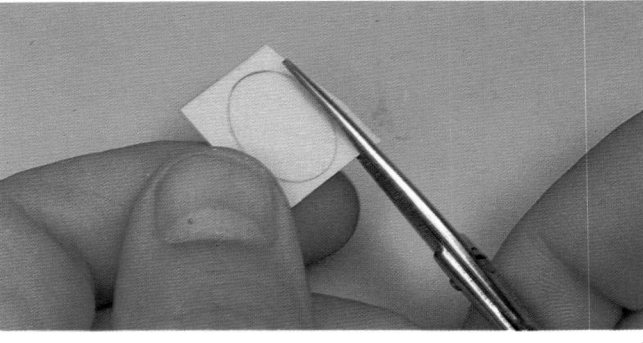

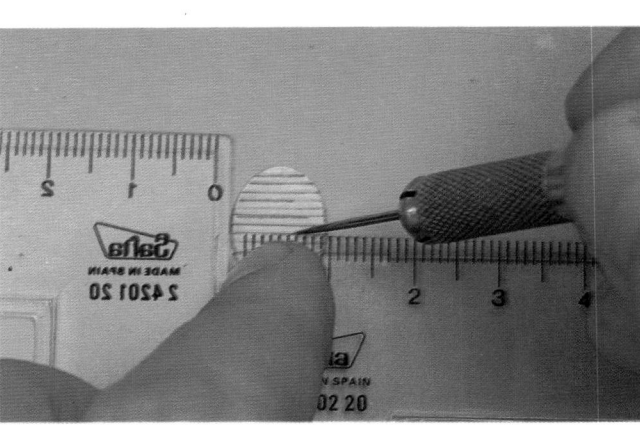

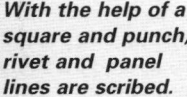

OTHER COMPLEMENTA[
ITEMS

The P-38 model we are buil[
basically accurate and do[
demand many changes. H[
some detail reinforcement [
airframe will improve it co[
ably. Fine mesh is inserted i[
air intakes to represent meta[
on the full size engines and[
extra detail is added to the [
gear.

Oval-shaped plastic card [
will serve to fill the holes in th[
lage booms. Measure their [
ters and find the nearest equ[
in an oval template sheet. O[
right size has been found, tra[
onto the plastic card and c[
blanks out with scissors. Prof[
sandpaper and draw detail[
scribed with a rule and [
Finally cut front and back p[
blank off the wheel well an[
them in the wells.

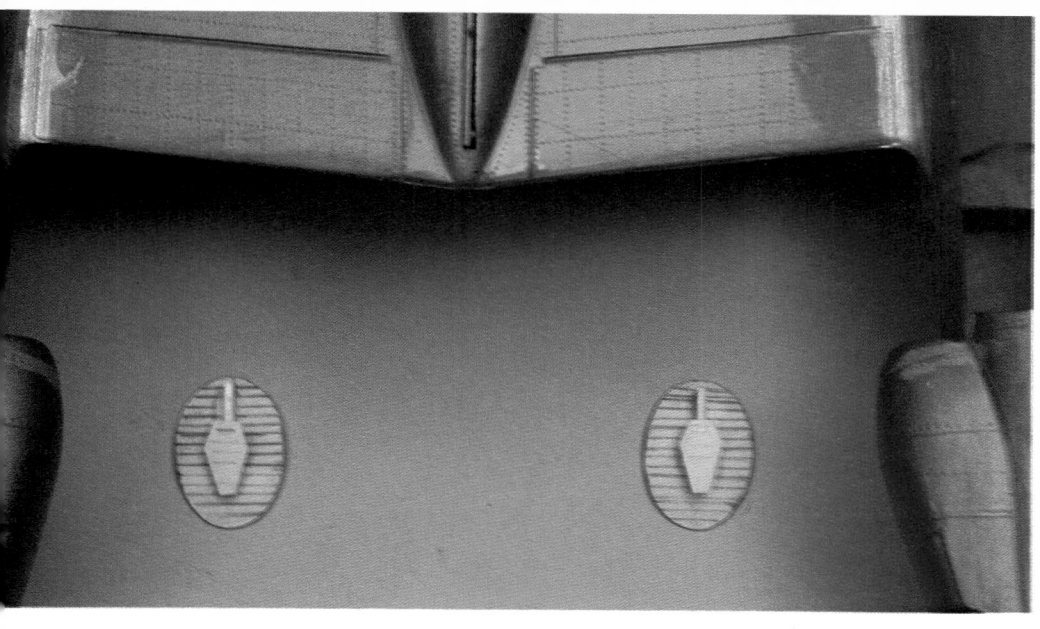

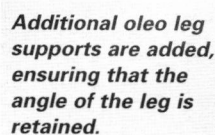

Additional oleo leg supports are added, ensuring that the angle of the leg is retained.

Drilling a hole in the oleo before positioning the hyraulic brake lines.

The thin metal line is attached to the wheel disk and secured on the inside of the wheel well.

The wheel well doors are rein-forced with short lengths of copper wire to prevent them coming adrift.

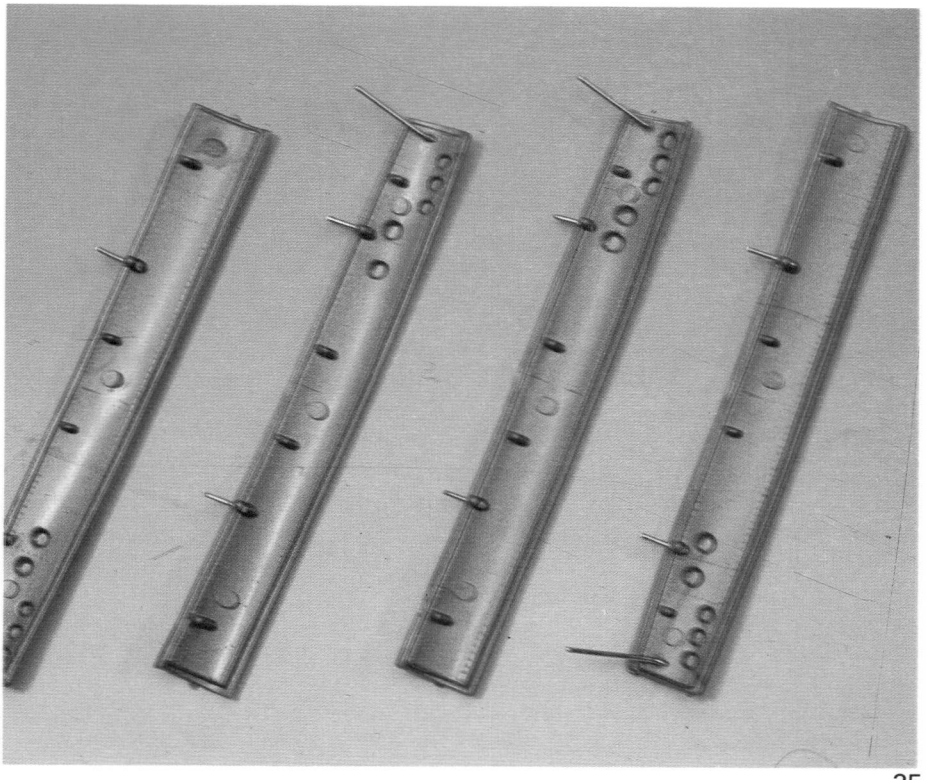

Paint the areas where the aluminium paint shows through.

All lower surfaces are painted with two coats of medium grey.

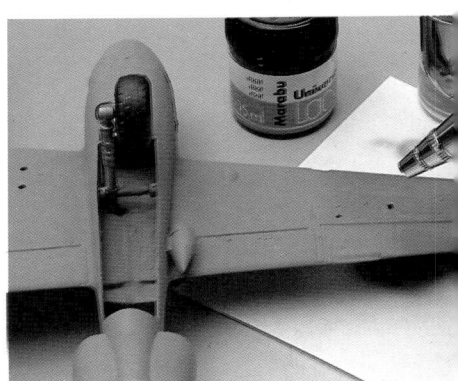

PAINTING A P-38 LIGHT-NING IN 1/48 SCALE

A model of this classic aeroplane of the Second World War represents a number of finishing techniques applicable to the type in general. Using hard and combined masking, plus freehand painting, a new scheme not suggested by the kit decal sheet is easy to achieve. The

subject chosen is a P-38J of the 401st Fighter Squadron, 370th Fighter Group of the 9th Air Force. On the model the finish will reproduce the peeling paint and general weathered appearance of the original, initially by painting aluminium areas where the camouflage paint has worn off. Maskol fluid is lightly applied with a toothpick to show the scratches as thin irregular shapes.

Once the cockpit has masked with tissue, the p phase starts. Using enam underside colour is prepa taking two parts of grey for e of white. The grey covers a surfaces except where the b white 'Invasion stripes' are These white areas are painte

Wings and fuselage sections are painted white, as

White areas are painted without masking.

White usually requires two or three coats to cover fully

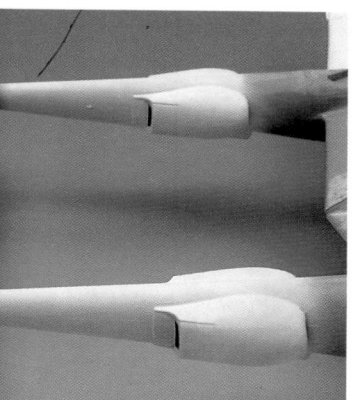

White is also applied to the vertical tail surfacesin the shape of squares.

Before applying the next colour, white areas are marked out with Letraline and masked off with adhesive paper,

faces where the white square ngs appear. All these light are carefully masked off with nd an adhesive mask before ng the camouflage colour. ut and apply a mask for the squares on each fin and and assemble and mask the ockpit components.

upper surface colour is a dark green obtained by mixing parts of olive green and one l grey. Apply the paint as two an initial light coat which is d to dry being followed by a ne. The soft demarkation line en the green and grey shades eved with an airbrush used nd although raised masks can d if required.

ow these guidelines and work and carefully when applying schemes that are a little ex.

Areas where paint will be shown peeling off are masked with Maskol. Only a thin application is required.

Hue richness

Although paint is usually app[...] a model in a single coat[...] perhaps some dry brush work [...] final stage, in this case some [...] tone has been added to the [...] colour. The objective is to ach[...] paint finish that shows up w[...] photographs. The model s[...] exhibit the various tonal diffe[...] as a result of weathering effec[...] surface fading from spillage [...] grease and fuel. A basic colou[...] is achieved by applying olive [...] to the base green with add[...] tonal values achieved by pain[...] soft, logitudinal bands towar[...] area where a faded blotch ap[...] A small quantity of white is ad[...] the second colour to paint th[...] surfaces, the sides of the [...]

Applying green on the sides of the engine nacelles over the greyish base shade requires care; the main fuselage and the booms need a wavy demarkation line with soft edges.

Use Letraline to mark out the areas where colour variation will occur.

To show where the paint has peeled. slightly folded masking tape is used to lift off the black paint.

When the mask is removed, a wel[...] defined white square remains.

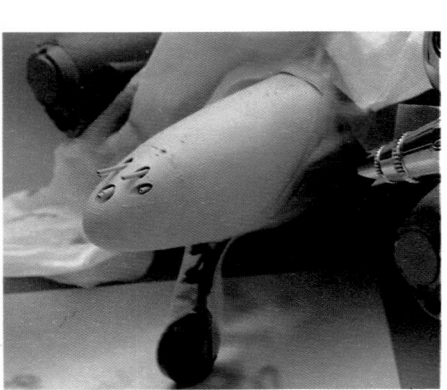

When the mask is removed, a well-defined white square remains. A mask for the yellow nose area is made with transparent adhesive paper. The dry base colours have a faded look as a result of tinting the paint.

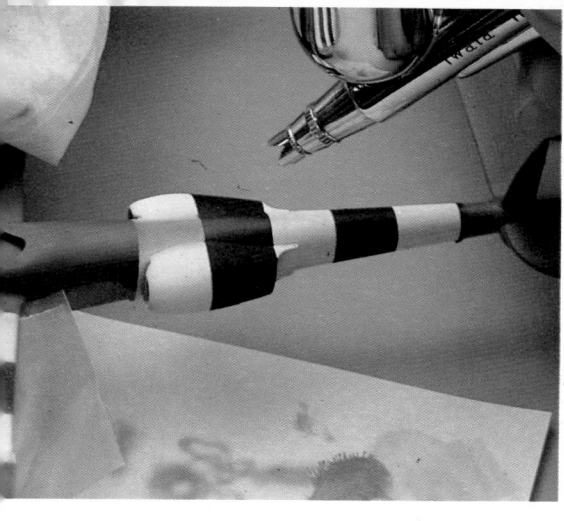

The superchargers of the P-38 soon resulted in exhaust burns along the top of the fuselage booms. White ink with sienna mixed in will reproduce this effect.

bright it can be dulled with a coat of grey to obtain the desired effect. The turbosuperchargers are painted matt black with a darker chocolate brown mixed with black applied with a dry brush to highlight detail. A last application is to airbrush a white-sienna mix to achive an authentic 'used' effect.

Finishing the propellers involves simply masking off the yellow tips and painting the blades black.

With the model painted it is ready to have numerous small stencil decals applied. Eliminating an excessive amount of whitish decal surround is one of the traditional problem areas in modelling. There is

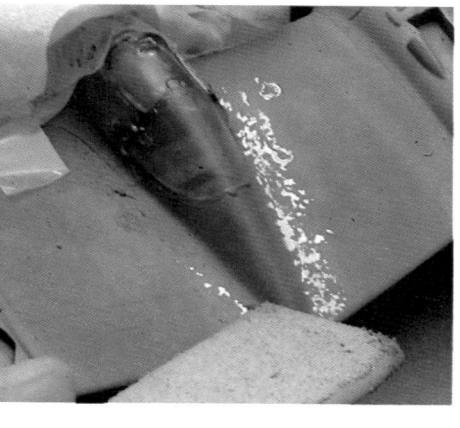

The best way to remove Maskol is with an eraser rubbed lightly over the treated area. When the masking agent disappears the aluminium surface is revealed. Treat this with a water-based green or grey paint if it appears to be too bright.

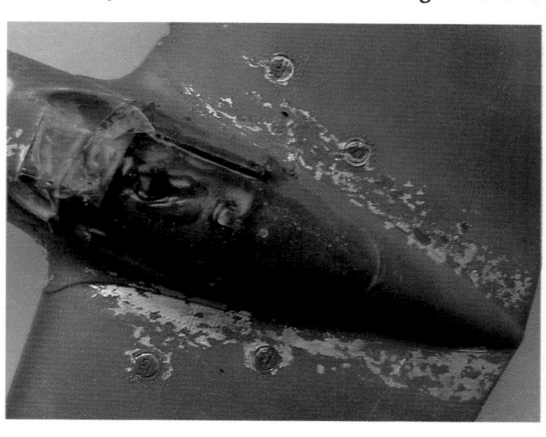

gs and the fuselage booms
ng the vertical tail sections.
re painting the black stripes,
ut with Letraline and protect
ite areas with
esive mask.
same
nose area,
f which is in
To give an 'opera-
look to the turbo-
rs, mix inks, one
aque white to three
na. Spray the tops of
oms from the turbo-
r housing almost to the
s. Use grey to highlight
bossed detail on the kit
astly, remove the
on the wings with an eraser
eal the aluminium skin
g through the worn camou-
aint. If the Maskol application
little too thick in places,
with a fine brush and green
If the metal appears too

Oil colours are very resistent to wear and can even be sanded and polished.

Peeling paint on the underside of the P-38's fuselage pod, the wing leading edges, the engines and even the propeller blades give an 'in service' look. To complete this weathering process, alumimium paint can be applied with very fine brush stokes.

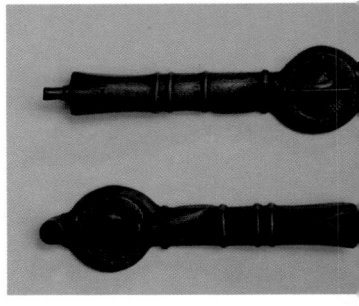

Turbo superchargers are painted l then dry-brushed in brown.

no complete solution as the problem tends to get larger as the decals get smaller! One way to overcome the problem is to use top quality commercial decals although some items may not be directly applicable to your chosen colours and markings scheme. Another alternative is to apply gloss varnish to the entire model or to those areas where the decals will go. Allow the varnish to dry, apply the decals and allow these to dry with the aid of Mirco products. Firstly use Micro Set which clears the adhesive film from the decal backing sheet, then use Micro Sol which softens the decal and allows it to fit very snugly even over a raised or indented panel line. One danger in using Micro Sol

is that the decal can completely wrinkle up. If that happens, leave it to dry out and the wrinkles should disappear. Applying all the decals to the P-38 takes time but once complete, a realistic model will result.

Because we chose an alternative colour scheme for this P-38 model some of the kit decals will not be used. To complete it, some alternative sources will have to be found such as 1/48 scale sheets of USAAF letters and numbers from Verlinden which have the advantage of being 'dry' decals which need no wetting. The best method of applying dry decal squadron markings is to rub each one down onto the model with a toothpick or other pointed imple-

The turbochargers are positioned their locating holes and finished using a white-sienna mix.

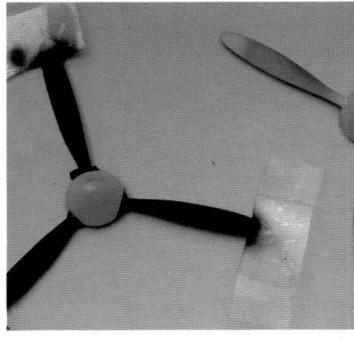

All propeller blade tips are yellow the rest painted black.

ment. Lift the backing shee and finally press the letter with a soft cloth. Press the de any joint line to prevent crac coat of varnish will keep eve in place.

The top surfaces are now finished with the peeling paint area, weathered camouflage and slightly dulled white stripes showing up well.

We used Verlinden decal sheets for our model. These are easily transferred by cutting out the required letters and rubbing them down on the model with a toothpick.

Rub each letter over gently and ensure that all of it comes away from the backing sheet without any corners cracking.

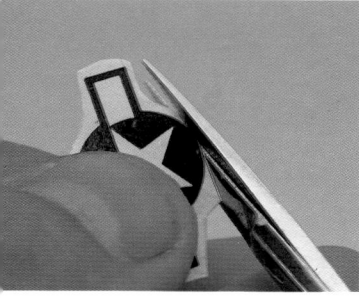

ch decal subject closely with scissors to prevent an unsightly rround appearing on the model.

Micro liquids complement decal application: Micro Set removes adhesive film while Micro Sol softens and prevents decals yellowing over time.

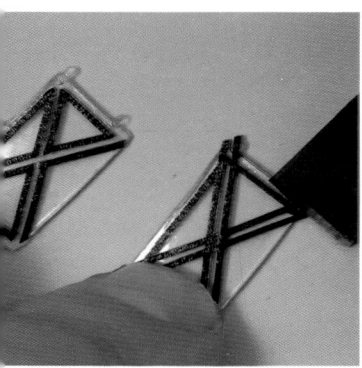

t framing can either be made by g painted strips of fine adhesive the tape is used as a straight ide for brush painting.

Use a fine pointed brush to paint the actual frame if this method is preferred. Several coats may be necessary to completely cover the transparent plastic.

Always hand paint with a fine pointed brush. Several coats of paint can be applied to obtain depth of colour.

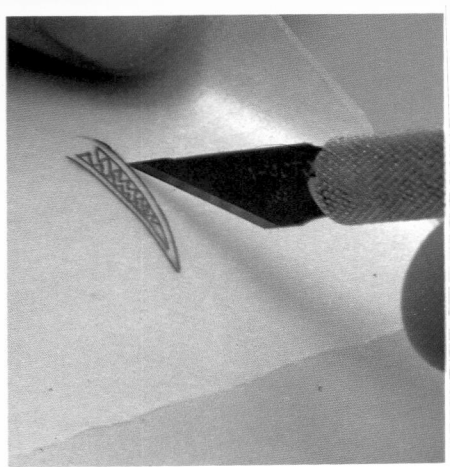

On this P-38 a thin sharkmouth appeared on the nose underside. This is drawn out and two templates are made, one for each side of the nose. Completion is in two stages using one of the templates for the mouth outline and one for the teeth.

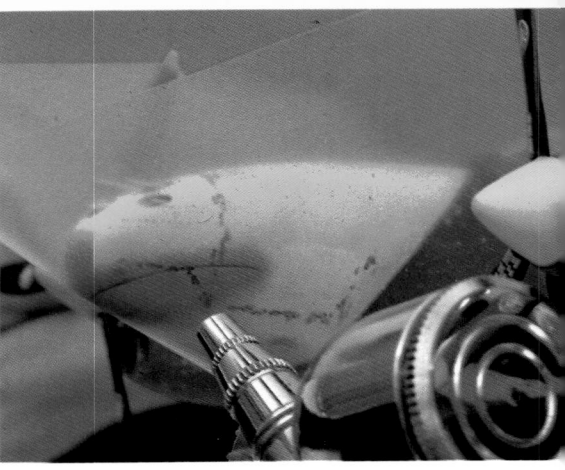

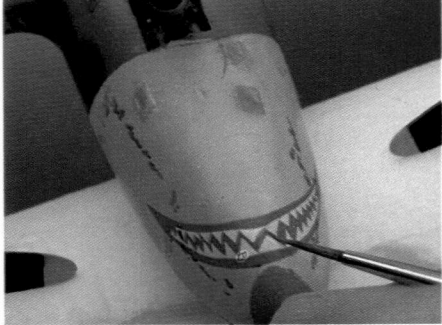

To join the mouth shape accurately, a fine brush is necessary.

A painted sharmouth does not have the problems that might be associated with applying a decal around a curved surface.

PAINTING AEROPLANES WITH A BRUSH

reat number of plastic modellers especially older ones, started by assembling aero-
e kits in series from manufacturers such as Airfix and Frog. Kits were mainly to 1/72
apart from those produced by Lindberg and Revell with their indeterminate scales -
ircraft of the Second War War soon emerged as firm favourites whatever the scale.
ing these models was something of a challenge as few specialised paints were avail-
e. The introduction of ranges of enamels was therefore very welcome and the first
ntically painted models began to be seen. Models were generally hand painted with
brushes, a technique that remains highly effective and more versatile than
many people might think.

FIRST STEPS IN BRUSH PAINTING

PITTS S2A

Civil aeroplanes and small light aircraft in particular are a little overshadowed by the massive interest in military types. There is however a number of fine models of light aircraft that can be built, many to 1/72 scale for ease of storage.

Painting a model with fuselage dimensions no greater than eight centimetres from propeller spinner to rudder is akin to painting a butterfly! Only microlights, which are also modelled in 1/72 scale, are smaller. The Pitts is from a small series from the Japanese LS range and these tiny replicas can look most attractive, particularly if a number of them are arranged together in a display case.

The fun thing about civil aeroplanes is the freedom of painting – if desired, paint schemes can be made up and applied without the restrictions governing military camouflage and markings.

Taking our lead from nature we

Tiny Pitts S2A in 1/72 scale from LS which includes small sport biplanes in its ki logue. All have very vivid colours which make a striking display, suitably differe other types of aircraft. Assembly is easy apart from the rigging.

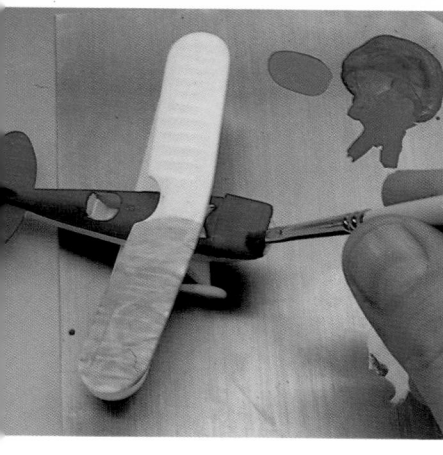

A fanciful colour scheme on an aircraft that can be 'owned' by the modeller.

The fuselage is painted in acylics in gradations of blue.

butterfly as our inspiration
nting the Pitts. Three shades
were chosen for the fuselage
llow and black for the wings.
vith a strong blue for the
half of the fuselage, adding
or the central stripe. More

white produces an even lighter blue for the lower half of the fuselage and undersides of the wings. Creating such a hue graduation involves a first coat with diluted paint to 'stain' the plastic. When this is dry a second coat is added to cover. The white

stripe separating the two colours is difficult to hand paint so a Letraline mask is used to complete the job properly.

First paint the stripe without worrying about how straight it is. Add the tape mask to cover the

stripe separates the two blues. Any shakiness can be
e by using a mask afterwards.

Letraline adhesive tape protects the white stripe.

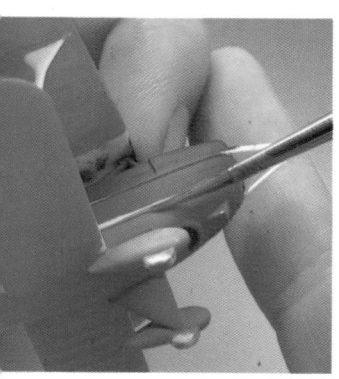

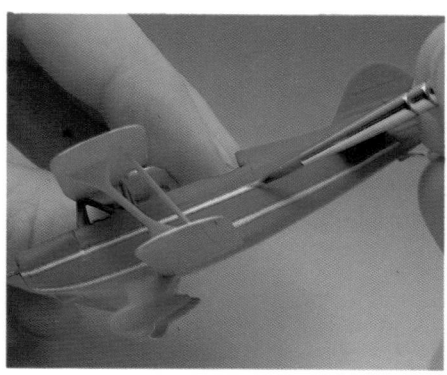

both the blue shades where
y.

Removal of the mask reveals a perfectly straight white stripe.

If any blue has encroached on the white stripe, retouch with a brush.

By mixing black and white, a medium grey is prepared for applying to the wing upper surfaces.

Yellow patches are drawn on top of the grey.

The patches are outlined in black.

Brush strokes have to be very neat and precise in this small scale.

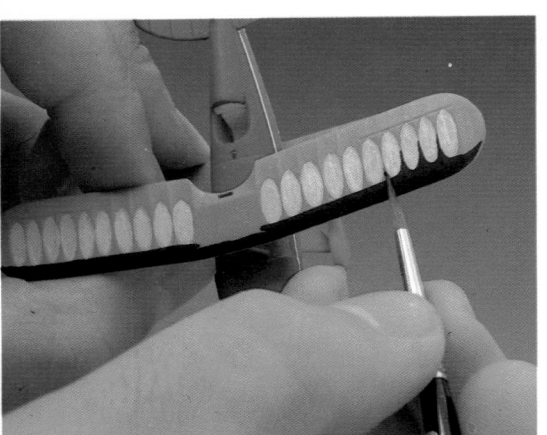

The entire lower surfaces of the fuselage and wings are in pale blue. The front of the engine is black and the propeller spinner is yellow.

colour, the second coat has brushed on with the strokes going in the same direction.

On the wings and rudd colours can be given a very li brushing to bring out the rib

white stripe and paint both blue shades up to the mask.

Paint has to be thin to prevent accumulation of paint at the edges of the mask.

Both wing upper surfaces are painted grey, two coats being applied using a No 2 brush with a good point. This brush is also used for the yellow and black decoration. Brush strokes should be even and continuous. The visible part of the cockpit interior is painted grey with the seat in mixed browns to simulate leather.

In order to retain uniformity of

A flat bristle brush used 'dry' is ideal for bringing out rib detail.

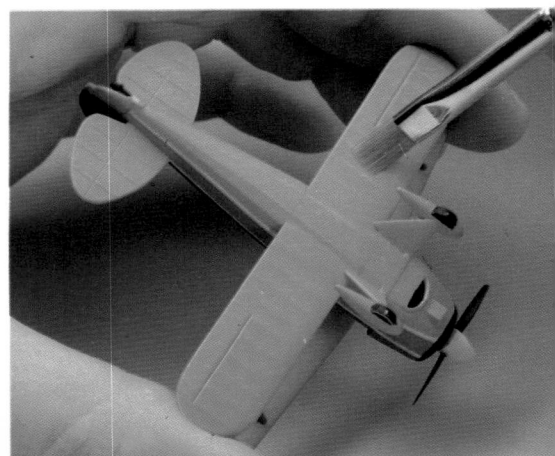

rigging
were fabri-
from plastic
the Pitts
them on the
or as well as
ng.

tion for deco-
models
incorporate
is to use
e decals, as
here.

All the colours used are acrylics, mixed to obtain the different colours required.

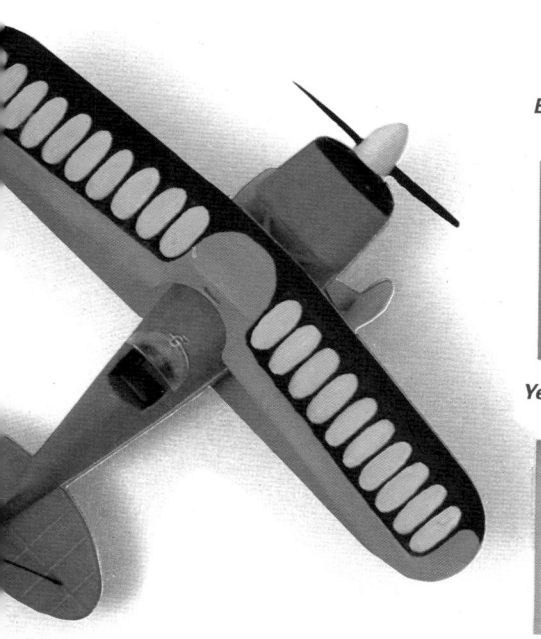

Blue + White 50%	*Blue + White 30%*	*Blue*

Yellow	*Black*	*Grey - mix White and Black*

A flat brush is used to paint large surface areas. Layers are applied with watered-down paint in two or three coats as necessary depending on the opacity of the paint.

To cover smaller areas, outlines are drawn and then filled in.

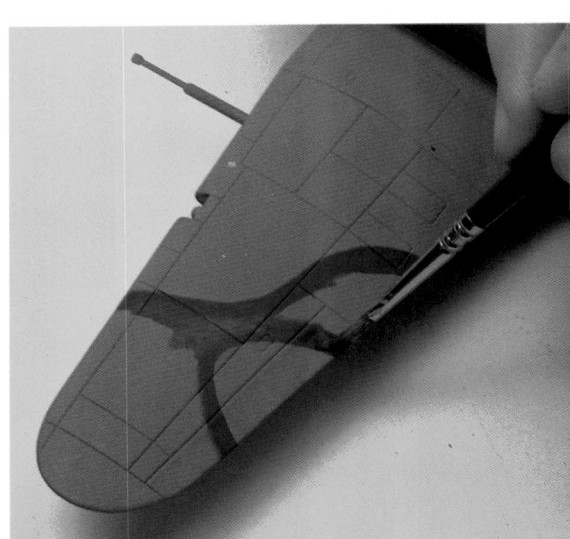

HAWKER HURRICANE MK II

The whole range of possibilities – and limitations – of brush painting is encompassed in the techiques employed on this model Hurricane. A 1/48 scale Hobby Craft kit, it has good surface and interior detail and construction is straight-forward.

The painting methods used here can be taken as a guide for many First and Second World War aircraft models and in general for any warplane that has undertaken combat sorties and been exposed to the effects of weather. One constraint we have imposed is to make camouflage demarkation lines sharp.

We started with a basic g mix of white, black and a amount of red, well blend colour uniformity. When ch the right brush to use, the ve quality is recommended. marten hair brush was use careful strokes in the same di ensuring that no brush appear. Two coats of pain

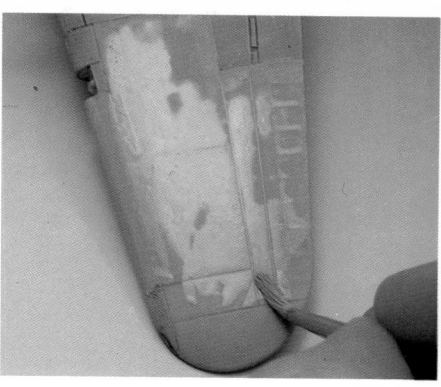

Painting with acrylic grey. Some acrylic paints are supplied with their own solvents which should be used for thinning.

...in coats of colour are applied in regular brush strokes, a perfectly flat finish ...result.

applied.

The first coat of paint is quite liquid but should cover the plastic well. The second coat is a little thicker (although not too thick) and in some areas, a third coat will be needed.

The second colour has a green

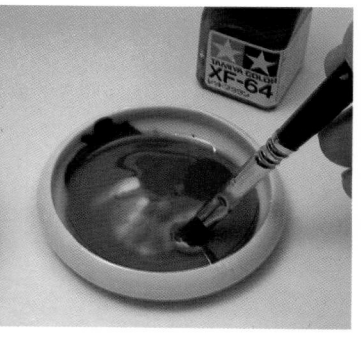

...al 'weathering wash' using ...enamel is applied.

Colour unifirmity should be evident throughout the entire surface of the model, avoiding any build up or patches. When using a brush, painting should be completed quickly to ensure even drying out over the entire surface.

hue obtained by mixing brown, yellow and dark olive green. As this colour is used for definite areas, the edges are painted first and then filled in, following the same rules regarding paint fluidity.

The entire underside of the aeroplane is painted in light blue which meets the camouflage on the wing leading edges and lower parts of the fuselage. The join line can either be painted freehand or masked with Letraline tape.

When applying light colours, any dry brush application will barely be seen so we used a very thin wash of brown enamel to simulate dirt on the wings.

When applying colour ensure that

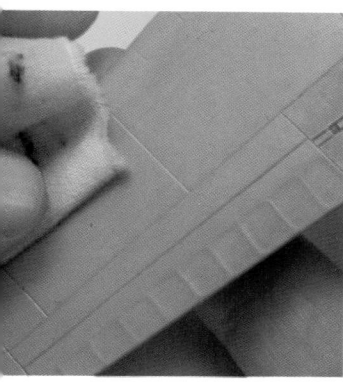

...e to ten minutes the model is ...over lighty with a clean cloth to ...e any excess paint.

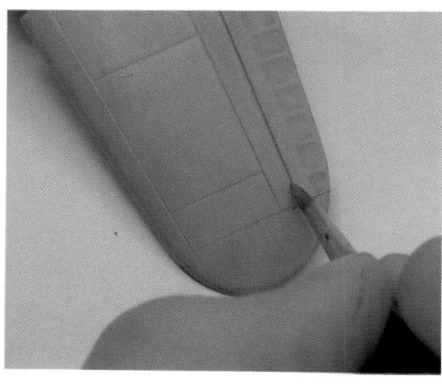

The ailerons and control surface lines can be picked out with the tip of a brush and very liquid paint.

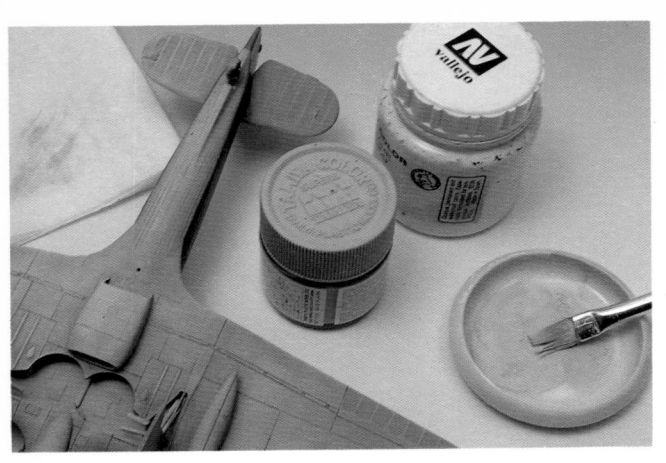

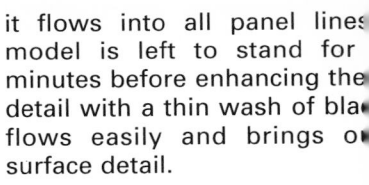

Once the base colours have dried, the dry brush technique is used to create wear. The grey has white added to it to give contrast.

it flows into all panel lines model is left to stand for minutes before enhancing the detail with a thin wash of bla flows easily and brings o surface detail.

Dry brush techniques

Once the first phases of painti complete, the dry brush techn employed, starting with the sides. The base colour lighter a small amount of white is u apply a light and realistic pa faded patches and streaks to

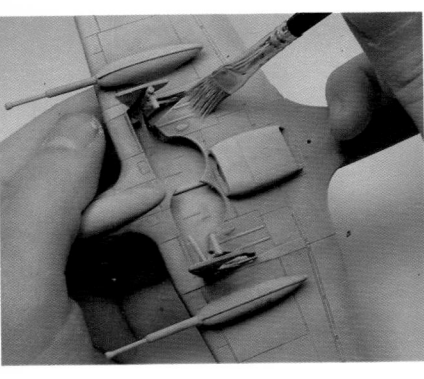

Concentrate on rubbing over those areas which will show maximum contrast.

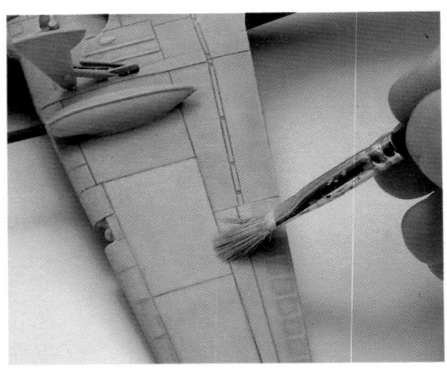

As the surface is rubbed over the scribed lines reappear.

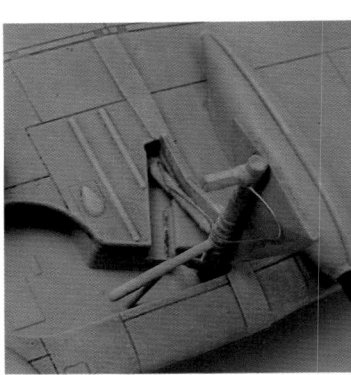

Thin copper wire is used to dtail t legs

late wear and weathering effe

Upper surface colours are with the dry brush in much th way, adding a lighter green original dark shade. Concentr the centre part of each camou section to maintain the de colour.

Similarly, the undersides a brushed over using the gre colour lightened with white.

Yellow is applied to Hurricane's wing leading edg as this shade does not cove three or four coats will prob required. Navigation light other small items are pain appropriate colours, red mix orange predominating. The is gloss varnished when al painting is completed.

The oxidization of the e pipes is reproduced by a dark and light browns. The fo for covering, the latter f brushing to bring out detail. B burn deposits can be crea black and brown washes buffing the base colour a there is a risk of the resul

Using both acrylic and enamel paints produces the desired results.

At least three coats of yellow will be necessary for this shade to cover effectively.

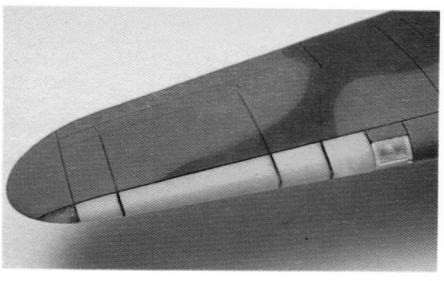

Lights will require two shades paint, with the brightest in the centre.

...h loaded with respectively light...
...reens and greys creates the worn

...ointing. An airbrush is there-
...valuable for these finishing
...s.

...ng paint

...lly 'age' the model, some
...d paint effects can be created,
...gh this is optional. All combat
...t exhibit some wear and tear
...gh contemporary photo-
...s will invariably show 'clean'
...l as worn examples. Much

The chipped and peeling paint effect is begun by painting small patches in black.

These patches are painted with silver (aluminium) paint, but leaving a fine black outline.

Variation of peeling paint is achieved by applying the aluminium directly without any black outlining.

it made mostly of wood, as in the Mosquito, or did it have a fabric covered metal framework as in the Hurricane? Knowing the answers to such questions will guide how we apply our weathering effects.

Weathing starts with black applied to those area where paint would logically have been worn away. Areas more worn have the black applied with the very point of the brush to give a typical scratched appearance. Later silver paint will be used to edge the black areas, leaving a thin outline of metal. Panels treated with aluminium only

...ds on the war theatre in
...the aircraft was operating:
...based machines and those
...from jungle airstrips tend to
...re weathered than those
...a long-stablished European
..., for example.
...ny event, peeling paint has
...ncorporated on our model
...ne. It helps here to have
...knowledge of the type of
...ction followed by the manu-
...r of the original aircraft - was

Blanking off the cockpit area with Maskol.

Remove the mask once painting is complete.

Although these worn areas look a little exaggerated, some full size aircraft were equally or more patched-looking. How much weathering to apply to a model is a matter of judgement and personal preference.

create a metal strike through effect, as seen on the full size original. These would include movable panels over gun and engine bays, the canopy runners and the pilot's foot and hand holds. Additionally, wing and tailplane leading edges and propeller blades all showed wear.

Decals

To reduce decal surrounds showing up against paintwork, these have been trimmed as close as po[...] They are placed with the h[...] Micro solvents and once the [...] have dried, the model is [...] varnished.

A general view of the Hurricane w[...] the necessary colouring complete[...] using enamel and acrylic paint se[...] rather than mixed.

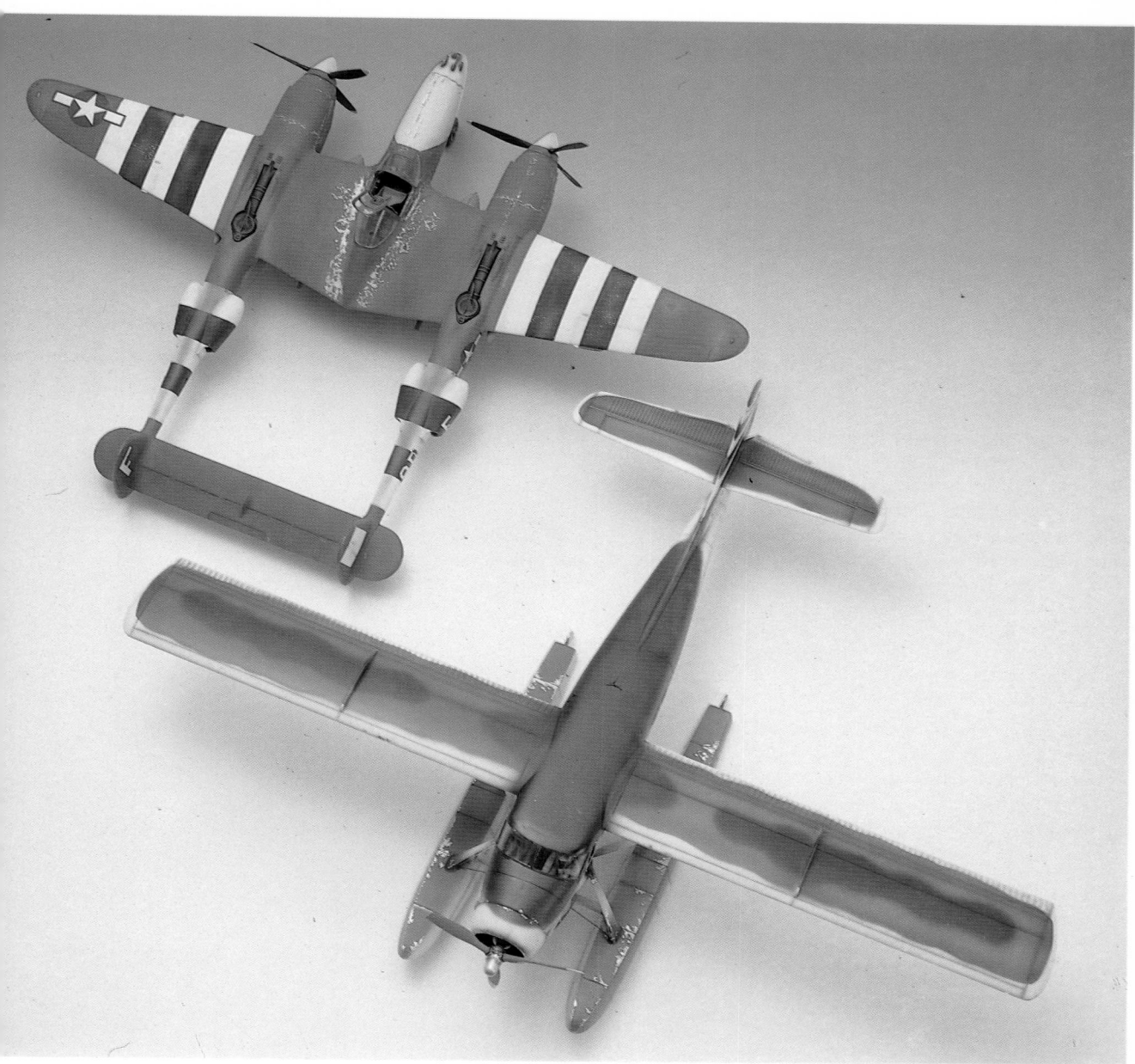

AIRBRUSH TECHNIQUES

delling revolution arrived with the airbrush. Painting methods improved significantly
d a model could be completed in much less time. Those finishes that were hard to
eve convincingly with a brush such as soft demarkation lines on camouflage and the
ttle effects common on Luftwaffe aircraft, suddenly became easy. Large flat areas
ere finished with a remarkable degree of paint uniformity, the expanding range of
airbrush-formula paints and inks offering vast possibilities.
s stabilised and an airbrush is now an indispensable and relatively inexpensive tool
modelling of any kind, limited only by the imagination and skill of the modeller. On
these pages are examples of the possibilities offered by airbrush painting.

SEAPLANE PAINTING WITH INKS

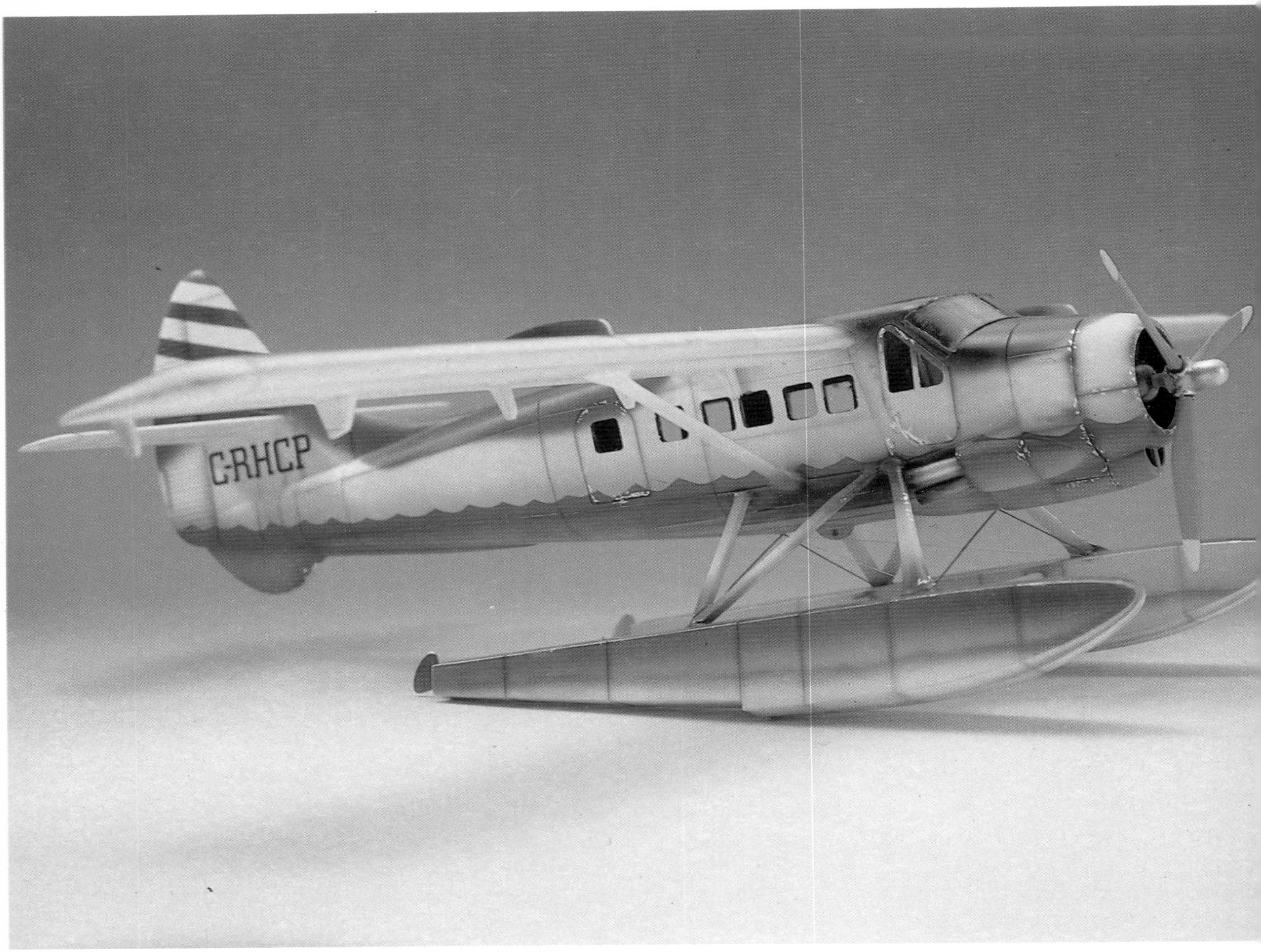

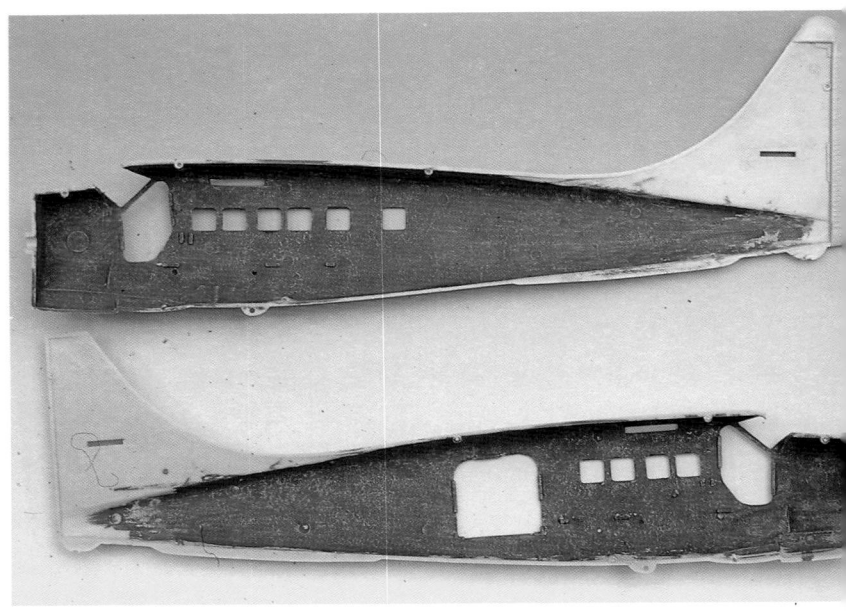

DE HAVILLAND DHC-3 OTTER

Originally designed for the Royal Canadian Air Force, the DHC-3 Otter found widespread civilian use by agencies such as the Spanish Natural Resources Ministry. The US Army also operated many Otters, the aircraft's extraordinary versatility making it a firm favourite where operations demanded an alternative wheel, ski or float landing gear.

As a model the Otter offers a range of military or civilian paint finishes and enjoying a certain freedom in painting we have imagined a Canadian bush pilot who, having fallen on hard times has emigrated to South America leaving his aircraft to its fate. The paint finish, already becoming scruffy through lack of attention, is gradually deteriorating.

The interior has been added to by some card sections and has been painted gre

...ts are very basic and cushions
...en added.

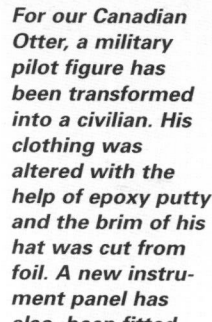

For our Canadian Otter, a military pilot figure has been transformed into a civilian. His clothing was altered with the help of epoxy putty and the brim of his hat was cut from foil. A new instrument panel has also been fitted.

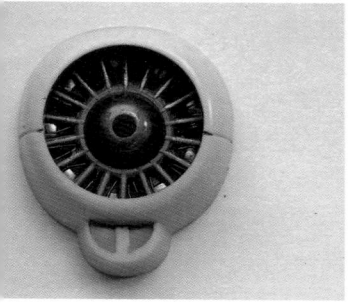

...he engine with copper wire and
...in the metallic blue.

...model used here is a Hobby
...t in 1/48 scale. Though well
...tioned, it lacks detail. The
...can be improved and the kit
...ent board is best replaced,
...from another kit or by
...-building a new one. The
...and windows can also be
...ed, some of these requiring
...r a good fit. As on all kits,
...kpit interior has to be painted
...joining the fuselage halves.
...as finished in green and to fill
...e rather bare cockpit, we
...ed the pilot figure by
...ng him with a hat.
...exterior was painted in a
...c blue which was obtained by
...silver and a small quantity of
...d blue. We found few prob-
...ith construction and once the
...main sub-assemblies have
...oined the painting can go
...In this case some less
...n modelling aids were used
...semi-opaque drawing
...coat of white acylic paint
...plied before using the ink.

General filling with putty and rubbing down. The floats require particular attention in this respect.

The airframe is coated in acrylic white before applying the colours.

55

In order to achieve a smooth
at least four coats will be ne
Each will build up the colo
satisfactory depth. It is advis
leave the model for twer
hours between coats.

Preparing the masks

Good results with an airbr
directly linked to correct n
and use of templates. Prep
begins with measuring thos
to be sprayed, drawing the
and transferring them as tem
Wing and tailplane templa
made first. As soft paint ed
required, a raised mask wi
preferably cut from card whic
better rigidity than paper. Toc
and small wedges are equall
for raising the mask two t
millimetres from the surfac
painted. Prussian blue ink wh
good non-fade qualities is
the darker colour.

The mask has to be helc
because the air source
airbrush creates a draught t

To decorate the Otter, inks in blue, green, red and grey shades are used.

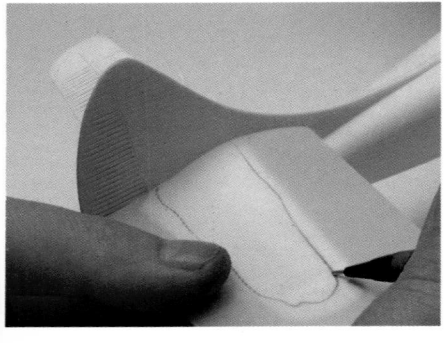

To prepare templates first draw onto the surface of the plastic.

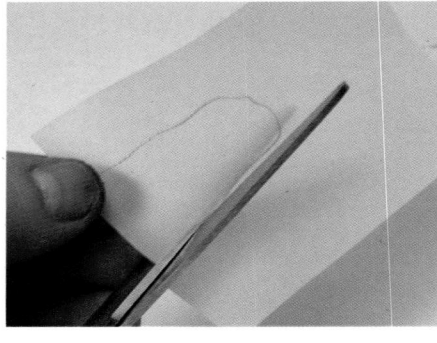

The drawing is tranferred onto firm transparent paper and the templates are cut out.

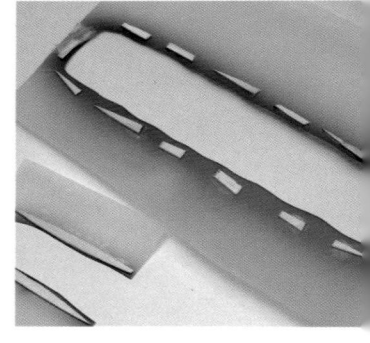

Toothpicks are glued onto the ma keep it away from the surface to painted.

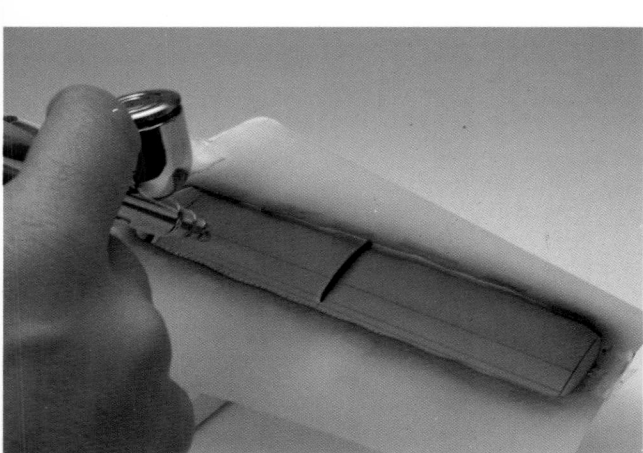

Paint in longitudinal lines, holding the airbrush the same distance from the surface.

tend to pull the mask away. N
tape with its adhesive
reduced is used. Colour is s
with the brush held perpendi
the wing and moved slowly
surface is covered. Suc
passes will strengthen the
and result in an even surface

Paint shades will gr
darken as the layers buil
allowing different shades
achieved where desired sin
varying the flow of paint fr
airbrush.

Once the desired paint

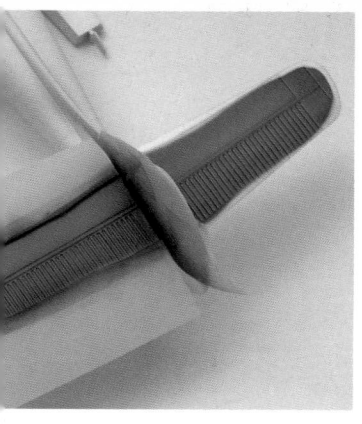

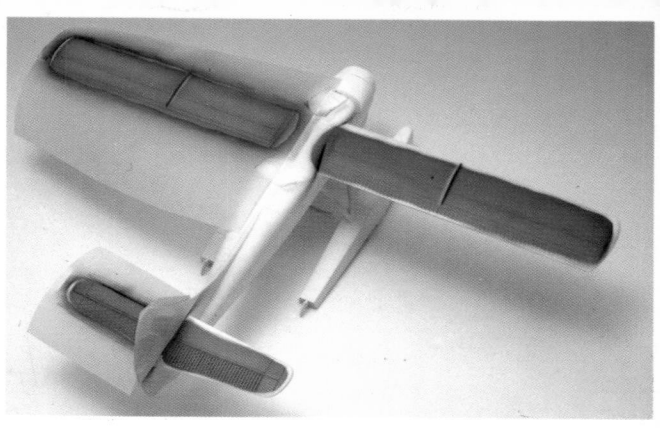

Uneven weathering of the tailplane can be achieved by concentrating on some areas more than others. Panels can be created by airbrushing up close and following the lines scribed into the plastic.

en achieved we move onto
ext colour, the dark blue.
 red to the lighter blue in a
tion of four parts blue to one
 creates the required shade.
ew colour is applied either
 freehand brush in a cloud

pattern or sprayed to give soft edges.

Before painting the fuslelage and tail, a mask is cut for the white rudder stripes. For this task, use masking tape cut to size and with its adhesive qualities reduced so that it

does not stick and lift the base coat. The entire fuselage of this model was painted freehand but a template similar to that used on the wings, can be used as desired.

Firstly paint the border of the patch, checking that the paint

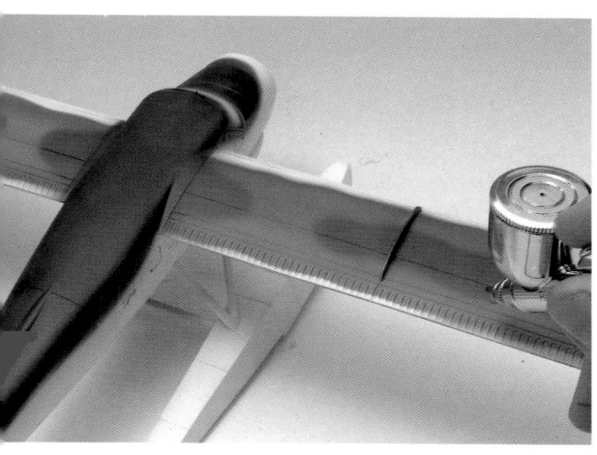

*al cloud shaped patch is created by spraying at a
 distance.*

The blue area of the fuselage is painted by holding the airbrush progressively closer on low air flow. Once the outline is done the rest of the colour is filled in.

*e mask is used for the scalloped edge on both sides of
lage before a green shade is applied.*

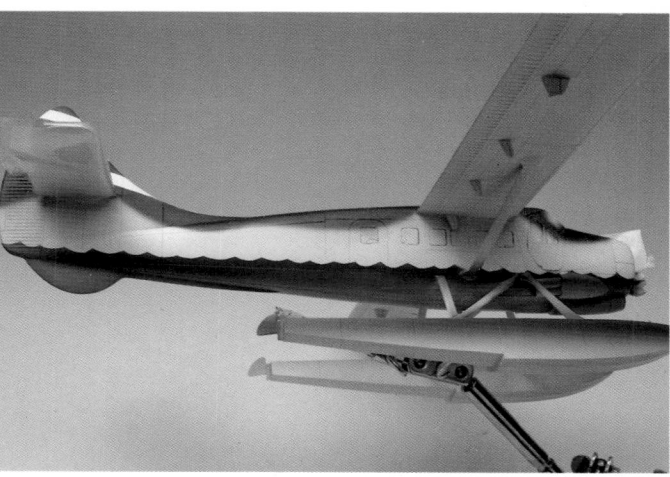

The floats are painted in gradations of green with the tops being the darkest.

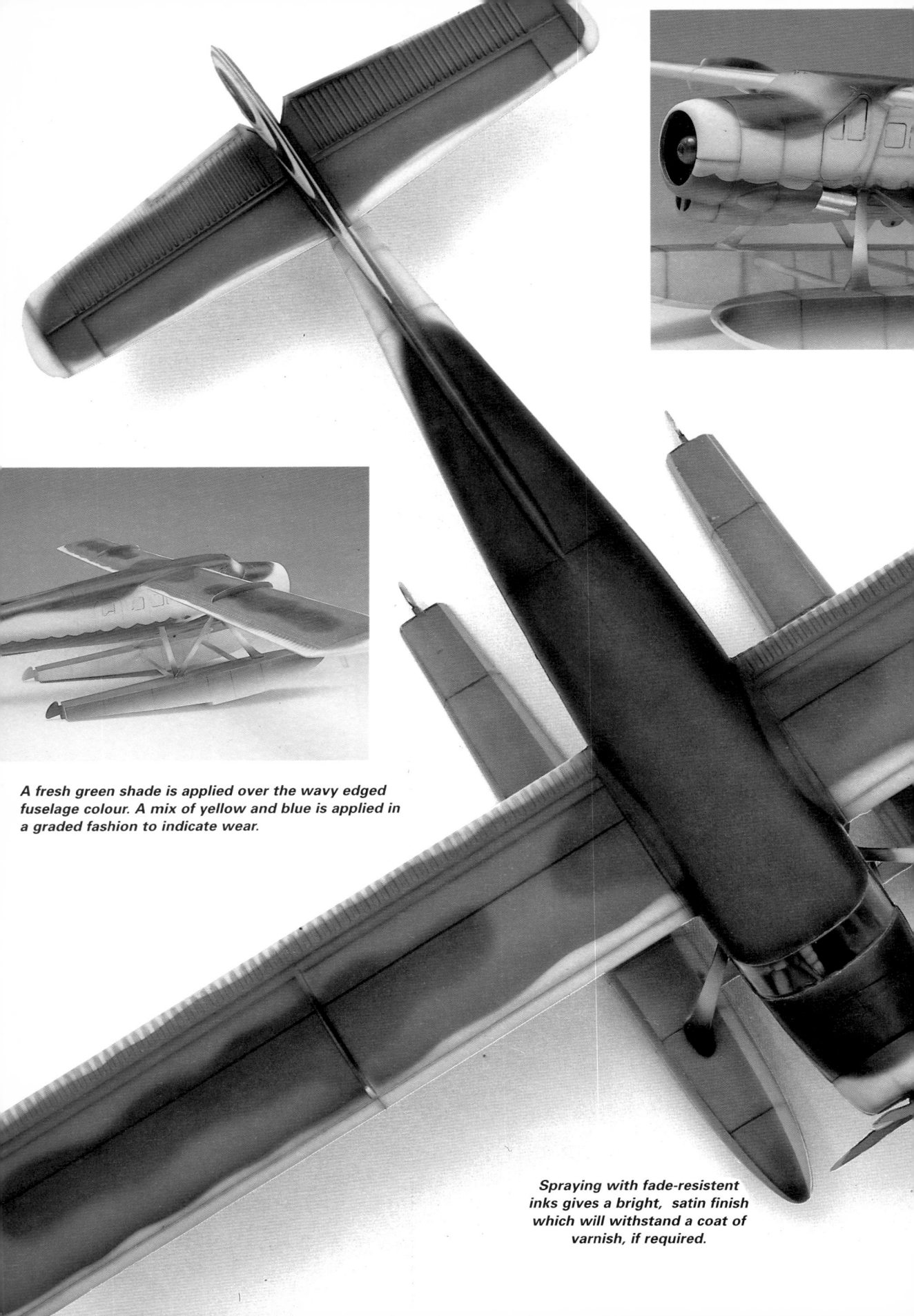

A fresh green shade is applied over the wavy edged fuselage colour. A mix of yellow and blue is applied in a graded fashion to indicate wear.

Spraying with fade-resistent inks gives a bright, satin finish which will withstand a coat of varnish, if required.

Every panel line is marked in grey with a freehand brush. In order to paint very thin lines with an airbrush it is necessary to get very close to the model and regulate the flow of air to that of the paint.

closest to the demarkation line remains thin. Once the outline has been done fill in the patch until it is well covered either with solid colour or with some visible variation, according to how much weathering is desired.

The lower fuselage is painted in green following the wavy line. A template for the scalloped edge is cut from adhesive mask drawing

The propeller hub and the exhausts are painted in aluminium acylic or silver ink from a felt tip pen, brushed on.

The exhaust pipes are dirtied with a mix of sienna brown and grey to achieve a burnt look.

paper. In this case a hard edge is required for affixing to the model so that spraying can be completed quickly. The floats of the Otter also require a gradation of colour, this being achieved by spraying with the brush held away from each float.

A lighter green is used for the wave effect on the fuselage sides

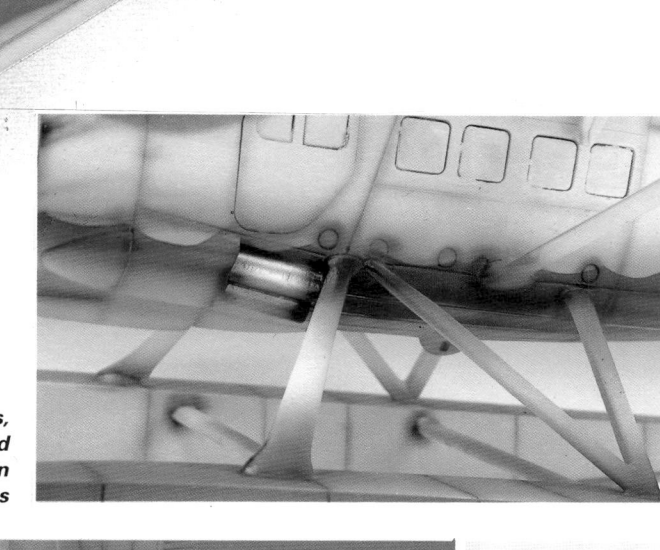

...wer surfaces, ...ing struts and ...are treated in ...same colours

Extensive wear on the lower fuselage is indicated by a light spray of sepia, graded to achieve the effects of water spray.

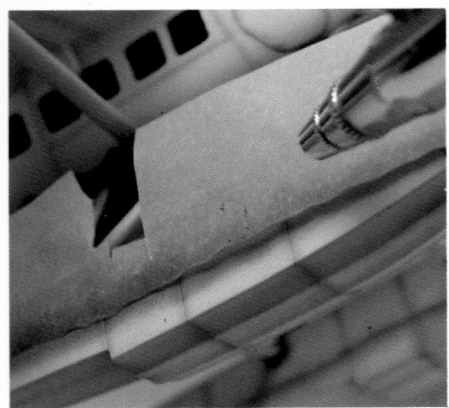

To replicate accumulated dirt on the floats, they are masked and sprayed in sepia.

The lower section of each float gets dirty, especially the areas that are in the water.

Faded aluminium is achieved by aluminium and silver paint.

and top surface. A mix of one part yellow to one part green is used in this finishing phase and we are ready to weather and dirty the aircraft.

The propeller hub and the exhaust are treated in silver.

The initial layer of dirt is applied in sienna ink to the exhaust pipes, propeller hub, the steps of the floats and panel lines. Grey is then used to enhance the panels, the elevators, fuselage detail, the rim of the engine cowling and the oil cooler.

The degree of deterioration shown on any model is a matter of choice. A well-used float-plane would have a generally faded look particularly around the floats, engine and doors. After painting is complete, the strut bracing wires are added.

General view of the finished DHC Otter complete with weathered finish.